Betwixt and Between
Life, Death, and Rebirth
Master Nan Huai-Chin

Translated by Pia Giammasi

Betwixt and Between: Life, Death, and Rebirth / Master Nan Huai-Chin ; translated by Pia Giammasi
Chinese title: 人生的起點和終站
Published by Nan Huai Chin Culture Enterprise Limited
www.nhjce.com
Copyright © 2023 Nan Huai Chin Culture Enterprise Limited
First Edition, First Printing

ISBN: 978-986-06130-9-4
Suggested Price: NT$220

TABLE OF CONTENTS

Publisher's note [Chinese version]

There are many kinds of books on life and death available, mostly from the Tibetan tradition. Not long ago, Mr. Hu Songnian made a special trip from the United States to Shanghai to ask Master Nan about life and death.

This book is a record of a series of informal talks by Master Nan for Mr. Hu and others. The explanation starts from death, and continues until birth, all in terms of the normal human life cycle. Although it is nothing more than the principles of Buddhism, it is not colored with religious sentiment and is explained purely from the standpoint of the science of life.

In addition, Master Nan also accordingly illustrates key points of practice and explains them from different angles so that students can easily grasp them, enter the right path of practice, and better understand the progress and direction of their personal practices, so as not to get lost.

Originally, the goal of religions was to seek the source or origin of human life, and each has its own explanation of life and death. Mr. Hu did not come all this way to seek answers for himself alone, but to also benefit those who wandered overseas, friends, fellow practitioners, and colleagues.

Generally speaking, monks leave household life to seek the answers to life and death. But lay practitioners also face life and death issues, so how could they not take these issues seriously?

This teaching is for lay practitioners in particular. There are quite a few people in the audience who have studied with Master Nan for many years. Therefore, during his explanations, Master Nan can seem sharp or harsh but this is meant to motivate and encourage them.

Master Nan originally did not want to print the records into a book, because he felt that the descriptions were brief and incomplete. However, most believe that, although the book does not meet Master Nan's standard of perfection, the deeper meanings manifest and are finely and clearly delineated. It can benefit the readers by resolving many of the questions in their minds.

This presentation was recorded on February 14th and 15th, 2006. It was recorded by Xu Hengshan, Zhao Yunsheng, Liu Yurui and others. Preliminary edits were done by Ma Hongda. The manuscript was edited by Ven. Hongren several times and Xie Jinyang did the final proofreading. The content summary was added by the editor.

Liu Yuhong

Miaogang

January 2007

Translator's Forward

This book is a record of Master Nan's talks in which he answered questions about death and rebirth.   In the modern world, both death and birth, more often than not, take place in a hospital rather than at home and so many people have not witnessed another human being entering or leaving this world. Many times our loved ones go through these monumental passages with only medical staff present. It is only through an understanding of what goes on during the transitions of death and rebirth that we can help others in the best way possible and prepare them or ourselves well for having children or to face death.

In secular terms, life is confined to the time between birth and death. Death is seen as the end of life, as if it were not part of life.   Therefore it is feared, it is sanitized and hidden away, almost swept under the carpet. Master Nan laments how death and dying are treated in the modern age.   When dying is recognized as just a phase of life, it is not so formidable. A person is considered dead when the heart stops beating and the brain waves go flat, but actually the process of dying begins long before that moment and continues on afterwards for quite some time. Master Nan guides us through the internal phenomena and processes of dying, from the earliest signs of the dissipation of the elements, to the point of clinical death, until the point when the consciousness leaves the body, which can take up to eight hours. With a better understanding of what is happening internally, we can more appropriately and respectfully care for the dying person.

Master Nan goes on to discuss from historical and cultural perspectives, the interesting customs, traditions, and superstitions in regards to funerals and burials, including earth, water, fire, wind, and sky burials. From this wider vantage point, ideas of right and wrong, good and bad, etc. can drop away leaving behind all of the unnecessary worry, effort, judgment, blame, guilt, obsessions, sanctimoniousness, and so on that can complicate or mar family relationships while making arrangements for the deceased.

Birth, death, funerals, and burials all happen within our world. We can see, hear, feel and know—to a certain extent—what is going on. However, in regards to what happens between death and rebirth, this is outside of the scope of human experience, and yet still imperceptibly overlapping. It is only those with deep spiritual attainment who can give us a glimpse into that realm. Within the various schools of Buddhism, one can find teachings on birth, death, the intermediate state, and reincarnation into various life forms. Those engaged in more scholarly study of Buddhism may be familiar with

Abhidharmakośabhāṣya, *Yogacarabhumi Sastra*, or Chinese Mahayana sutras describing the intricate details of these phases and processes. In general, Western Buddhists learn about the intermediate or *bardo* state from teachings on the book, *Bardo Thodol*, better known by the name given to its first translation, the *Tibetan Book of the Dead*. Master Nan talks about the intermediate state from first hand spiritual knowledge giving a unique window into the intermediate state of existence just ever so slightly outside of our range of perception.

Buddha's teachings on pregnancy and birth are not commonly known. The Buddha gave detailed descriptions of human birth starting from conception, outlining all of the changes that take place week by week over the nine to ten months of pregnancy. Since these ancient Buddhist sutras written in terse classical Chinese can be very difficult to understand, most people are not familiar with them. Master Nan makes these teachings accessible and correlates them with modern terminology and knowledge.

Through an incredible mixture of personal stories, deep meditative insight, history, science, and Buddhist teachings from the Pali Canon, Mahayana sutras, Yogacara, Vijnanavada, and Chan, Master Nan guides the reader through death, the intermediate state, and rebirth into the human realm.

Pia Giammasi doing oral translation for Master Nan during classes at Taihu in 2006

Acknowledgements

I would like to thank Andrew Nan and TH Lee for supporting the publication of this book. Beyond the financial support, you both give me invaluable moral support and encouragement. One couldn't ask for better Dharma brothers!

As well, great thanks to the Nan Huaijin Culture Foundation in Hong Kong, to the Heng Nan Institute in Shanghai and the many devoted individuals of the Heng Nan's team who work tirelessly behind the scenes to help carry Master Nan's vision forward. Heng Nan Institute's magnificent buildings and grounds are home to the largest collection of Master Nan's original calligraphy, and hold classes, meditation retreats, conferences, and other special events. In commemoration of the tenth anniversary of Master Nan's passing, the Nan Huaijin Memorial Hall will be inaugurated at the Heng Nan Institute. The founder of the Heng Nan Institute, TH Lee, felt that, in addition to the inauguration of the Nan Huaijin Memorial Hall, it would be propitious to have some English translations of Master Nan's books come to print and therefore this book and other translations are being published.

Heng Nan Institute in Shanghai

Mr. TH Lee Founder of Heng Nan Institute

The translator, Pia Giammasi, next to the statue of Master Nan created by Chan Wen-Kuei, which was unveiled at Heng Nan Institute in Shanghai on Master Nan's hundredth anniversary in 2018.

Session One

Temple in New York

Eastern Esoteric Buddhism, Tibetan Buddhism, and Bon

The monk from the army, Ven. Xianming

Before and after life

The scientific nature of cause and effect

Life and death through change vs. life and death in sections

We are all "transformation bodies"

What is enlightenment and Buddhahood?

● Changing and unchanging

Four main principles

Master Nan: Dear friends, today I want to talk about something which is actually a very serious topic and all of mankind has pursued answers for thousands of years to this question of life and death. The impetus for this discussion was from our old classmate Hu Songnian, who lives in New York, USA and has studied Buddhism for many years. Speaking of New York, there is a famous temple there, Chuang Yen Temple, built by Judge Shen Jiazhen, a native of Hangzhou, Zhejiang.

Hu Songnian: His ninety-third birthday is this month.

Master Nan: Oh, he's ninety-three! He was prodigious in the aviation industry in his day, very famous. He is of the same generation as Dong Haoyun, the father of Tung Chee-hwa (former Chief Executive of Hong Kong), and Yang Guanbei, the father of Yang Lin. After he arrived in the United States, he did an extraordinary thing for the Chinese people. He gathered many scholars and translated Chinese Buddhist scriptures into English. This is almost forty or fifty years ago, when I was still in Taiwan.

Later, when he discovered that New York did not have a Buddhist temple, he started to build a Dajue Temple. Most of the money was paid by him. At that time, it was a very big temple in New York. He invited many monks from Taiwan who were originally from the mainland. Then later, he invited some monks and lamas directly from China. When I was teaching class at Yang Guanbei's, he said to me, "Teacher, you'd better go." I laughed and said, "I don't like going to foreign countries. There are many talented people, they don't need me there."

Shen Jiazhen later built Chuang Yen Temple, which is a very large temple in North America. I have been invited there many times. I haven't seen him for decades, nor did I meet him when I was in the United States. There is an old monk in Chuang Yen Temple, named Master Xianming, from the northeast. This monk was part of a real historical story during the war of resistance.

Around five or six years into the War of Resistance against Japanese Aggression, it was discovered that the Japanese were playing tricks in order to defeat China. Esoteric Buddhism is divided into Eastern Esoteric Buddhism and Tibetan Esoteric Buddhism. Indian Esoteric Buddhism came to China during the Tang Dynasty, but by the Ming Dynasty, the Chinese didn't like it very much, so it went to Japan. Koyasan in Japan is entirely a tantric sect. In Chinese academics, the general name of these schools is Eastern Esoteric Buddhism (東密 Dong Mi). Many Chinese spell writing, mantra practice, and ghost hunting are related to Eastern Esoteric Buddhism. Chinese orthodox culture hates this stuff, but India and Tibet are more accepting, and Japan also.

The Tantric Buddhism in Koyasan, Japan, originally only had male monks, and women were not allowed to go up the mountain, which discriminated against women. Later, there was a Japanese woman who wanted to go to the mountains to practice, but the monks in Koyasan absolutely refused. The woman was very unconvinced, and outraged, she built a hut at the foot of the mountain to practice, and later became enlightened. You see, women in the world are really amazing! Seeing her success, Koyasan is now open and women can go up.

The Esoteric Buddhism that took root in Tibet is slightly different from Japanese tantra. It was passed to the Han area in the Tang Dynasty. There are the Nyingma School, Sakya School, Kagyu School, Gelug School, also known in Chinese as the Red Sect, Multi-colored Sect, White Sect and Yellow Sect. The Dalai Lama and the Panchen Lama are Gelugpa. The Black sect, which you may have heard of, is not Buddhist. It is an ancient religion focused on incantations called Bon, which existed before Buddhism entered Tibet.

Let's return to the War of Resistance. We found out that when the Japanese fought, they asked the Tantric Buddhists of Koyasan to do vanquishing practices to help defeat the Chinese. In response, during the sixth year of the War of Resistance against Japan, in Chongqing, the Nationalist government requested a ceremony of "Protecting the Country and Relieving

Disasters." It was a big Buddhist ceremony to protect the country and to reflect the energy of Japan's magic spell back to them. At the time, two masters were invited to perform the ceremony. One was the great Chan Master Xuyun, who was to preside over the mandala of the orthodox Buddhism; the other was Gongga Hutuktu, the living Buddha of the White Sect, who was to preside over the mandala of Tantric Buddhism. They are both my Shifus[1] with whom I took refuge. I have Shifus with whom I took refuge, Shifus who taught me Buddhism, a Shifu under whom I became a monk, all kinds of Shifus. I took refuge with many masters. Back then, when I was studying Buddhism, if I saw a practitioner who had some level of attainment, I would take refuge with him. I did not always learn Dharma from those masters, I just wanted to create a karmic connection, which is a type of empowerment. There are many types of empowerment in Tantric Buddhism: empowerments to create a karmic connection, empowerments of transmission, wisdom empowerments, all kinds of empowerments.

This is just small talk before we begin our class. We had mentioned Master Xian Ming of Chuang Yen Temple, he must be over ninety years old now. It was because of me that he went to the United States. In Chongqing, during the "Protecting the Country and Relieving Disasters Ceremony" presided over by

---

[1] teacher/master/mentor

21

Master Xuyun, I met the monk called Xianming. I liked him at first sight. He really looked like a monk, tall and majestic with a perfect face. What does a perfect face look like? Just like Master Xuanzang's great disciple, Master Xu Ji, and Master Xuanzang himself, very dignified.

At this time, the Japanese had already retreated towards Burma, and the British were in a sorry state. China organized a youth army whose motto was "One inch of mountains and rivers, one inch of blood; one hundred thousand youths and one hundred thousand troops." They were recruiting members and students above middle school stopped studying and came out to fight the Japanese. Yang Lin went to Chongqing and joined the Youth Army. Many small events in history are actually big junctures, but most of them have been forgotten by everyone.

While helping out during the Protecting the Country and Relieving Disasters Ceremony at Chongqing's Lion Mountain, we chatted with the two masters when they were free. There was also Dai Jitao who was chatting with him at the time. He was the revolutionary veteran of the Kuomintang, followed Mr. Sun Yat-sen, and also took refuge with Master Xuyun and Gongga Shifu. One evening during a conversation, I remember that they were talking about how young people across the nation wanted to save the country. Everywhere there were people joining the youth army, Catholics and Christians were going. However, they hadn't heard of any young Buddhists or monks who were willing to participate. It seemed rather embarrassing! Monk Xianming said, "No Buddhists are going? Then I will go." So Monk Xianming went to join the Youth Army. At that time, the director of the General Political Department of the Youth Army was Chiang Ching-kuo. And so we parted ways.

A few years later, I started lecturing in Taiwan. As for the two large temples in the United States, Shen Jiazhen asked a monk to go over and be the abbot. For some reason, he left within a year and the next one left soon afterwards as well. Not sure why they left or what the problem was but it was very difficult. People say that Shen Jiazhen's wife is very rich, but very thrifty. I was told that after using paper towels, she would not throw them away, but would stick it on a window pane. After they dried, she would take them off and use them again. She was so thrifty, so rich, and so good at doing good deeds.

Later, I was teaching at Shifang Academy in Taipei. Someone told me that there was a layman, Lei Yuting, from the Northeast who taught Buddhism and gave excellent lectures. I said that I don't remember hearing of him when I was on the mainland before, so please find out more about him. Later someone said he knew me. I said, "I don't have a lay friend named Lei Yuting from the mainland but since he said he knew me, either I could go see him, or he could come to see me." He said, "He doesn't dare to come to see you, he is afraid." I said, "Why?" "He is afraid that you will look down on him." I said, "That won't happen! I will have to go see him."

In the end, he came to see me one day. When I saw him, I said, "It is you! You are Monk Xianming! Back then you were the head monk after Master Xuyun." He was the one who helped the Master and was equal to the dean at a university. I said, "I didn't know that Layman Lei was you, why didn't you come to me?" He said "I didn't dare, for fear that you would scold me." I said, "You sacrificed yourself for the country, you gave up being a monk, joined the youth army, and now you teach Dharma. I respect you, why would I scold you?" Then he told me that he lives on Yangming Mountain, and he doesn't interact much with the Buddhist world. He thinks Buddhist people will not understand him, and look down on him for disrobing and becoming a soldier. In fact, he went to save the country. He is the lineage holder of the Tiantai School.

Later, I said, we are old friends, you can come and teach here. I invited him to come and be a lecturer. I asked him what he wanted to do in the future. He said that Buddhism in China was in a poor state, Taiwan as well, and he wanted to leave. I asked him where he wanted to go and he said, Thailand, Thai Buddhism was flourishing. I said, do you still want to be a monk? He said, of course! I am a layman now, wearing ordinary clothes, but I will put on robes when I arrive in Thailand. However, it is not easy to get into Thailand, and I have been applying for several years without success. I said to him Thailand is no fun, go to the United States! He said that he would like to go to the United States, but there's no way. I said there is a way.

He has a very good female disciple who has served him until now. He must take her if he wants to go. When you hear this, you might be thinking that there is a problem with a monk taking a woman along, but I don't think that way. She was so respectful to him. With their difference in age, it was like a father taking a daughter. He was not in good health. This woman was not married, and it was a great opportunity to learn Buddhism from him. I said "Two people, I'll do it, I will help you out right away. That is the best way to spend money!" As soon as I put out the word, friends helped, and they were off to the United States. They are still at Chuang Yen Temple.

How did we get into all of this? I got carried away! It all started from layman Hu Songnian, who is a standing committee member of the Chuang Yen Temple. In New York, many overseas Chinese study Buddhism. He also mentioned yesterday that a group of overseas Chinese practice the Cundi (Zhunti) Method and want me to give them an initiation. Now to answer you, I won't go to the United States again at my age.

I want to invite Master Xian Ming back, but he won't come either. He originally said that he did not dare to return to the mainland because they thought he was Kuomintang. How could they say that! He sacrificed himself to save the country! He said that he worked as a political instructor under Jiang Jingguo under the Political Department. Oh, I said, I was also a political instructor as well. Don't worry about the Kuomintang or Communist Parties. You should go back to the mainland. There is no one in the Tiantai School. [No lineage holder] Don't you want to bring the Tiantai lineage back? He said, I'll go if you go. I said I will definitely go back. So I'm back now and want to invite him back, but I really dare not. He is in his nineties, I too am old and if an old person has to take care of another old person, how agonizing!

Layman Hu has been communicating with me for many years. He is very stable and honest, and he often asks questions. He writes well, and has good opinions. Yesterday he said that after so many years of correspondence, we could publish a book. He asked me to see what should be published and what should not be published. I haven't had time to look. He comes back to see me every year and talks about many issues face to face. His most recent correspondence mentioned the issue of life and death, because he read the "Tibetan Book of Living and Dying" and the older book, "The Secret Method of Liberation During the Bardo Stage," which talk about how to help people attain liberation when they die and other such topics. These two books are now available in English. People here don't pay much attention to international knowledge. The research on death and cognition in America all started by these books.

Christianity says that when people die, there will be a final judgment by God. Buddhism does not say this, nor do the Chinese have this view. The soul is reincarnated. Originally Western culture did not accept reincarnation, but now things have changed. It is more generally accepted, and people want to know more about it. People have gone to Southeast Asia, Myanmar, Thailand, Cambodia, and Tibet in order to do research. I believe there are many cases of small children saying that they were a certain person, in such and such a family, and I have been reborn in your family. Now the Americans are starting to investigate such cases. If they find such a child, they take him back to his previous home. The child tells where his things can be found, and, indeed, they find the objects where he says they are. In one case, the child recognized his former wife. The old lady didn't believe it until the child whispered something in the old lady's ear that only her husband could know. "Whaa!" The old lady starts crying, "He really was my husband!"

Based on the documentary, the story was later made into a movie, some of which was accurate and some not. This is to point out that this is a current international trend. Americans are now studying life sciences and cognitive sciences, studying whether the human soul has a past and a future, whether there is karma. In other words, traditional Western culture, Christian culture, does not believe in karma, the cause and effects of past, present and future lives. Now everything is changing, and it is being explored, which definitely has to do with the "Tibetan Book of Life and Death." Anything which has to do with Tibet is popular because Tibetan Buddhism is very mysterious. This is not to say right or wrong, only that this is a phenomenon.

The issue of life and death has long been studied by Buddhism, Taoism, and Confucianism. For thousands of years, the Chinese have believed that there are past lives and future lives. What is called "soul" can be called "bardo body" in Buddhism and it is also known [in Chinese] as the "interim body." This knowledge existed thousands of years ago. Why is it called the "interim body?" After we die and the "soul" has left this body, before the next life, this part of existence is in the interim, so it is called the interim or bardo body.

Actually, strictly speaking, we are living within an "interim body" now, because this is not the ultimate state of being. I will say more about this point. Buddhism talks about different kinds of life and death. There are "divided life and death", and "life and death of change." I often ask, what is the foundation of

Buddhism? "Three-fold cause[2] and effect, and the six paths of reincarnation within samsara" is the foundation of all Buddhist studies. This is meta-science. Many people don't understand Buddhism at all, and are just talking nonsense! They don't believe in karma either, and only have a very rough idea of karmic retribution. In fact, karma is anytime and anywhere. Without causality, nothing in this world could be established. Law, politics, economy, medicine, architecture, food, men and women are all within the web of karma.

Catholicism, Christianity, and Islam also talk about retribution. Those who do good things go to heaven, and those who do bad things go to hell. So, who is in charge of this retribution? Who is judging? Buddhism does not agree that someone will judge you for your sins and sentence you to hell and heaven. Why does Buddhism not agree with this? Because of the principle of cause and effect, the laws of karma. It is a meta-science. Going to heaven or to hell, the six paths of reincarnation, and three-fold karma are all our own doing. We study Buddhism in order to understand what it is that is governing life. This ability to govern one's own fate is not something you can do now, and therefore that is the focus of spiritual cultivation.

---

[2] Three-fold cause and effect is the karmic relationship of past lives to the present life and of present life to future lives.

I have studied philosophy and religion all my life, so why do I focus on Buddhism? Chinese Confucianism and Taoism are the same as Buddhism, but things are not as clearly explained as by the Buddha. The Buddha has cultivated enlightenment and knows that all sentient beings, all life, and the entire universe have a common origin, which is beyond creation or destruction, and is unchanging. In philosophy, this is called "ontology." The six paths of cyclic existence, divided life and death, are just the manifestation of change within the original nature.

Let's assume that time is eternal. In science, when you use the word "assume," it means you are ready to get down to business. Why do I say the word "assume"? Because time is not necessarily eternal. Assuming that time is eternal, then yesterday, today, tomorrow, the past, present, and the future are just divisions of "eternal time." Dividing time into segments is an artificial, intellectual idea.

Our life is the same as this principle, from the standpoint of so-called original nature, time is eternal and unchanging. It's just that in one "life" we may be a man and in the next a woman; women seek husbands, men seek wives, and then have children and later die. Yesterday, today, and tomorrow, every minute, every second, life—physical and mental—is changing, the universe is changing. This is what is called "life and death cycles of change." For example, I like to joke about something which is also the truth. Many students who have not seen me for decades say, "Teacher, I haven't seen you for more than 20 years, you are still the same!" I say, "If I was the same, wouldn't I be a strange old monster?" In fact, I have been changing all along and am not the same. This is life and death.

I often quote Confucius saying to Yan Hui in <u>Zhuangzi</u>, "Brushing shoulders, everything is not as it was." How can we understand this? The current education will not help you to understand this. You cannot understand it unless you start your learning using classical Chinese. Brushing shoulders means that two people brush shoulders or arms as they pass by each other, or have some sort of short interaction. As you and I go past each other, in that short amount of time, we are no longer the same; everything has changed. Change is that powerful.

Among Buddhists, the Theravada Arhat believes that he has ended his cycle of life and death, that the practice of this life has been successful and he will no longer be reborn. Actually, they have, at best, ended the "cycles of divided life and death (分段生死)." The Mahayana Bodhisattvas laugh at them for their small-mindedness. Not come back? Not possible! Even if you enter samadhi for eighty-four thousand kalpas, you still have to come out of it. Therefore, it is not the ultimate, that only a Great Bodhisattva can become liberated from the "life and death cycles of change (變易生死)."

31

Hu Songnian asked me last night whether Buddha Shakyamuni is a transformation body. Correct, but what is a transformation body? In terms of Buddhism, all the Buddhas and all Bodhisattvas in the ten directions and three generations are transformation bodies, and all of us living beings are also transformation bodies. There is only one constant center, represented by the central Vairocana Buddha. All Buddhas are transformation bodies of Vairocana Buddha. All sentient beings are also transformation bodies of Vairocana Buddha. In other words, all are variations of the functioning of the original nature. And this original nature, this origin of life itself has never moved. So in this life of Shakyamuni where he became a Buddha and spiritual leader, he is also a transformation body. Amitabha is also a transformation body.

Before discussing this subject, we must recognize that the entirety of human culture, be it Chinese or Western, and all fields of inquiry have developed in pursuit of the answers to life. In universities, the many courses, research institutes, fields of study such as economics, sociology, political science, physics, chemistry, applied technology, etc. are all related to life inquiries. If it has nothing to do with life or survival, the field of study would not be established or would naturally be phased out. All of the phenomena within survival, we call life. For the sake of life, whether we do business or become an official, we spend so much money on our children's education to get bachelors, masters, and doctorate degrees. In my opinion, and maybe I am not right, studying, earning money, or becoming an official and all that jazz are all life issues.

India had religion before Buddha Shakyamuni. What are now called Nepal, Pakistan, Bangladesh, and Afghanistan were originally considered parts of ancient India. Buddhism later spread widely, not only throughout the entire Indian subcontinent, but also to East Asia, Southeast Asia, Central Asia, and even Europe, but only part of it. India's borders and landmass were very large, but it was not unified in ancient times. There are more than 60 kinds of languages and writing, which until now have not been unified. As well, they themselves do not pay attention to history. If India had gone through a unification process like China did during the Qin and Han dynasties, and had unified its writing, it would be a powerhouse.

This illuminates what is precious about our Chinese culture. Starting in the Qin Dynasty, we unified our writing and made an effort to preserve history and culture well, including Buddhism of course. Even now, we can still read ancient books and understand the thinking and writings from thousands of years ago. However, with the popularity of vernacular writing and simplified characters, we have almost lost the keys to open the historical and cultural treasure house. This is a big problem.

India does not have a unified script and doesn't place importance on history. After the Arab and British invasions, India was left devoid of Buddhism and the Sanskrit script of today is not the same as ancient Sanskrit. The real content of Indian Buddhism came to China along with the Buddhist scriptures. I lamented with some Indian friends who practiced yoga, saying that I really want to restore the treasures of your ancestors! They said that we also want this, but words alone are not enough. I said that your ancestor Sakyamuni Buddha, was such a great saint. His entire legacy has been preserved in China. If it weren't for China, it would all be gone now.

Ahh, language! Two thousand years later, there are still so many dialects in various parts of China, there is no unity of spoken language. The northerners cannot understand southern dialects such as Cantonese or Hokkian. The so-called cross-strait dispute involves language and communication issues. It is necessary to have standardized language. Of course, dialects should not be done away with, the two can coexist.

I have gone off topic again. Well, since the cultures of the world have developed in pursuit of the answers to life, of course China is no exception. You all want to study Buddhism, to what was the Buddha enlightened? Why do we want to get enlightened and become Buddhas? To put it bluntly, it is still to answer the question of life, to investigate the ultimate foundation of all life in the universe. This naturally also includes the issues of life and death, and survival. Under the Bodhi tree, the Buddha attained great enlightenment, and he obtained the "Annutara Samyak Sambodhi". This is a Sanskrit transliteration. When translated into Chinese, it means supreme, unsurpassed, unequivocal enlightenment; supreme, unsurpassed, unequivocal knowledge, and supreme, unsurpassed, unequivocal way.

What is Bodhi? It is enlightenment, understanding. The attainment of Bodhi is not mere intellectual understanding, rather it knowing with your entire (mindbody) being. "Annutara" is the supreme and complete; "Sambodhi" is supreme, unsurpassed, unequivocal enlightenment and supreme, unsurpassed, unequivocal knowledge. Awakened clarity anytime and anywhere without any confusion. "Samyak" means right or correct and unequivocal equanimity, ultimate equality.

In the Diamond Sutra and in other sutras, it says that becoming a Buddha means attaining "Bodhi," why? To put it another way, the great enlightenment of a Buddha is knowing the origin of all life in the universe. Within Chinese culture, Chan Buddhism upended all those terms calling it, "realization!" Realizing what? A great Chan master of the Tang Dynasty said that he realized "THIS!" When asked what "this" was, "Dry dung! Dog poo!" he answered. Be it shit, THIS, Annutara Samyak Sambodhi, God, Lord, spirit, they are all just names. It is impossible to explain the truth of life, so it is merely called Bodhi.

In his one lifetime in this world, in his so-called enlightenment and becoming a Buddha, what was Shakyamuni's realization? It is complete and total knowing, not through logic, knowing that the essence of all life is beyond creation and destruction, that there has never been any birth nor death. This is what he realized and became a Buddha. However, Buddha Shakyamuni was born into this world and later he died and left, just like us. This is the phenomenon of life. The cycles of divided life and death are like yesterday and tomorrow, the day after tomorrow, or last year, next year, past, present and future. Liu Xiyi from the Tang Dynasty has two famous lines, "Year after year, the flowers are similar; Year in, year out, people are different." The truths within Chinese Buddhism are encapsulated in these two sentences. Life is like this. Every year there is a spring, and every year there is a winter. This represents the two ends of all phenomena, coming into being and fading into demise; thoughts, cells, and all matter arises and ceases, always like this. Finding the foundation of the existence and extinction of life is called becoming a buddha, or the attainment of bodhi.

In other words, the Buddha said that all sentient beings, not just humans, including the physical material world and spiritual world of the universe, are phenomenal changes of this original nature. They are all cycles of divided life and death, and all are life and death. Change is not the ultimate, not the root, but the phenomenon. But the overall functioning of life is beyond time, neither life nor death.

Why was Buddhism so easily absorbed into Chinese culture? This is because the Book of Changes (I Ching/Yi Jing) from the ancestors of Chinese culture, also referred to similar ideas. The Book of Changes has several main understandings—the changing, the non-changing, intersecting change, and simple change. The so-called "non-changing," there is something non-changing, without genesis or death, the fundamental unchanging essence. "Changing" means life and death, and changes. All phenomena in the universe arise, are ever changing and then desist. There is nothing constant. The relationship between men and women, the relationship between father and son, will definitely change, and the constant is not called affection. "Intersecting change" means that within the changing, there are intersecting changes, cross overs, and intuition. This intersecting change is called 'yoga' in Sanskrit, mutual intuition, correlating changes. "Simple change", all complex changes come from simple changes. Only understand the complexity, but not the simplicity; or only understand the simplicity but not the complexity, both lack full understanding. The changing, intersecting change, and simple change are all inseparable from their origins, which is the non-changing. (According to the second volume of Wei Shi Shuji:

"What is called yoga is also known as being in resonance.")

This cornerstone of Chinese culture mixed with Taoism, Confucianism, and the various ancient schools of thought; then, Indian Buddhism and the understanding of the Buddha's awakening was absorbed and integrated and it all became "Eastern culture."

Therefore, when talking about religion I often say to Westerners, where in the world does your religion come from? You know, the five leaders are all Orientals! Confucius, Laozi, and Buddha Shakyamuni are from the East; Jesus and Muhammad are from the Middle East, which is also East. There is no Westerner among them. You Westerners vehemently oppose the East but in fact, most of your cultural ideas came from the East. The five masters all understood this one principle, but their methods of preaching and dissemination were different, according to local conditions. Of course, realizations of truth have varying degrees of depth, and the most thorough teachings are given by Shakyamuni Buddha. The Chinese Book of Changes also has this truth.

For example, in the Eight-Eight Sixty-Four Trigrams of the Book of Changes, there are principles, however, the rules are always changing. You want someone to tell your fortune, but what can be told? It's useless. When the prediction is right about this matter, things change and it becomes wrong. Things can change at any time, so there is no absolute accuracy. It is like "looking for the first mark of carving on a hewn boat or searching for a sword which fell to the bottom of the ocean." People often say: Teacher, I'm going to do business, can you use the I-Ching to do a fortune reading for me? I said, it will either be success or failure, there is no middle. You want to make money doing business and have made the initial investment. So if you didn't make money, but you didn't lose money either, does this count as 'middle?' You lost time and energy, so you already lost! You said that you did make money. What you had earned is gone, and so in fact, you did not actually make money. Everything is in the process of transition. This is the truth of life. This is a big principle. Therefore, learning Buddhism, Taoism, so-called meditation and zen, achieving great enlightenment, is the realization of the origin beyond birth or death. This is Buddhist study, and also the Chinese Taoist school of cultivating immortality.

I often say that after examining the cultures of the world, East and West for a long time, you find that Chinese have a unique culture that no other has. They dare to assert that one's life can be "immortal." Only the Chinese Taoists dare to say that. Recognizing that one's essence is neither born nor dies, one can practice to become immortal like one's essence. After eliminating death, one will live forever. Taoism calls this state,

"Having the lifespan of heaven and earth; resting with the sun and moon." "Having the universe in hand; all metanoia arise in the heartmind." It's only the Chinese who have the courage to make this scientific assumption that life can last as long as the lifespan of the universe. The universe is active and in this great void, activity never stops or rests. Our lives also keep it alive forever.

The Buddha is different. The Buddha knows that the essence is beyond life and death, but does not talk about extending this lifespan. Although China's Chan and Esoteric Schools do not address this issue directly, they hint at the question: when Buddha Shakyamuni attained Tao, why did he leave? The Buddha said I did not leave! I'm still here. And the most interesting thing is that, before he left—the Buddha left at the age of eighty-one—he first told his cousin Ananda, who was a monk, and Ananda did not say anything. At the end, when Buddha announced to everyone that he was leaving, Ananda knelt and, crying bitterly, said, "Nooooo! You can't go!" The Buddha said: I deliberately asked you three times, and your words were to determine my fate. I could have stayed in this world and not die. I asked you to see if it was better for me to stay, or pass away? I asked you three times, but at that time, you were trapped by Mara, and your mind was so clouded that you didn't answer me. If you say stay, I would have remained. You didn't say anything and now this opportunity has passed. Mara then beseeched me not to remain any longer. I will fulfill Mara's wish and leave. However, it is recorded in the scriptures that the Buddha behest four of his disciples—Venerable Kassapa, Venerable Rahula (Buddha's son), Venerable Pindala, and the other is Venerable Kundapadhaniyaka—to retain their physical bodies and stay in the world, to extend their lifespans in this world. It is said that Venerable Kassapa is still entering Dharma at Jizu Mountain (Mount Kukkutapada/ChickenFoot Mountain) in Yunnan. This is called "Retaining Form and Remaining in the World." These things are all materials for studying life. The study of life and deep principles (道理 Dao-li) of life are that profound.

Speaking of deep principles, let me first explain that our Buddhism teaches "Dao-li," and now China's Christian preachers also use the term "Dao-li." "Dao li" is a term inherent in Chinese culture, which Buddhism and Christianity both borrowed and interpreted. The Noble Sūtra of the Explanation of the Profound Secrets (Ārya-saṃdhi-nirmocana-sūtra) divides deep principles (道理 Dao-li) into four types: the principle of observation, the principle of action, the principle of proof, and the principle of Thusness.

The principle of observation (觀待道理): All physical and spiritual phenomena are within this range. They are all relative phenomena arising through causes and conditions, for example:

flowers, plants, trees, earth, rocks, water and fire; all kinds of life and everything in nature; houses, furniture, all kinds of electrical appliances built by humans; countries, nations, society, laws, politics, economy, ethics, military, medicine; our thoughts and emotions; words spoken, the articles written; natural sciences, humanities and studies. Within the term, principle of observation (觀待道理), "待" means to be in a state of relative existence, arising and desisting from causes and conditions, or we can say, arising and desisting as the fruit of karma.

The principle of function (作用道理): All material physical and spiritual phenomena have their own functions. For example, eye consciousness, ear consciousness, nose consciousness, tongue consciousness, body consciousness, and mental consciousness each has its own application; the eyes, ears, nose, tongue, body, brain, etc., each organ also has its own purpose; earth, water, fire, wind, air, awareness , and consciousness, each element has its own function.

The principle of observation takes a different perspective, from the perspective of phenomena. All material and spiritual phenomena arise from causes and conditions, the fruits of karma, and they exist relative to each other, not alone or absolute. In other words, every phenomenon will inevitably transform with changes in causes. The principle of function is from the perspective of function. All phenomena and all factors have their own use, in other words, each has its own changing applications.

The third type is the principle of verification and attainment (證成道理)which is both personal and scientific verification. Verification of what? Verification of Suchness, truth, the original truth. In an instant, there is purity; thoughts and troubles are gone; and one is no longer obstructed by the physical body. This is "kungfu" (the results of time plus effort). Verification is the quest for proof and is scientific in nature. This is called the principle of verification and attainment.

The fourth type is the principle of Thusness. (法爾道理) Thusness does not change with the transformations of causes, conditions and effects. It is the original nature. It does not arise or desist, is neither tainted nor pure, and does not increase or decrease. This term, "Thusness," was created when Buddhism came to China. Chinese people usually talk about "Nature," or the way things are. But why not call it Nature? So why is this principle not called the principle of Nature? For fear of falling into a materialistic concept, or a Taoist concept or a non-Buddhist Indian philosophy of "natural." So another name was created—the principle of Suchness. The so-called principle of Suchness doctrine is an unchanging truth, a matter of course which cannot be overturned.

The things we talk about generally and casually are within the principle of observation and the principle of function, are all observable, logical and have their functions. Of course, many things people talk about are illogical, and they still fall within the principles of observation and function. Scientific research falls within the principles of observation and function, and principle of verification and attainment. Researching the principle of Suchness is also within the principles of observation and function. As for the principle of verification and attainment, it is a personal process of spiritual practice and verification within one's own life. It is successful verification through right thought and reaching the attainment of Arhat, Bodhisattva, or Buddha for example. This is the principle of verification and attainment, within which are also the principles of observation and function.

Behind these principles is the highest principle of Thusness, which is the ultimate truth and is unchanging. It cannot be said to not exist before verification and attainment. It has never changed. If it changes at all, it is not Tao. When you really verify and attain Thusness, we call it "attaining Tao" but this is just a way of speaking. It is a way to say "observing the truth," because "Tao" has never left you. Not even a smidgen has been gained or lost. Zen Buddhism uses an analogy of returning to one's original nature. After which, various wondrous abilities are initiated. At that point, the principles of Thusness, function, and observation are all perfectly integrated. This analysis of these theories is also the principles of observation and function. It is a convenient means to help rid you of confusion.

Session Two

"Passing away in one's own bed"
The end of life in different time periods
People who pass away without illness
Material and spiritual life
Changes in the Four Great Elements before death
Signs of the direction of reincarnation
Five types of no-consciousness

Master Nan: Now we will formally begin the session speaking about the phenomenon of life and death. Note that we will only talk about the normal life and death of human beings.

In my life, I have spoken about the topic of life and death so many times that I am sick of it. I don't like teaching the same topic again and again. When I taught a course in school and had to repeat the same class, every time I taught it differently. I am loath to repeat the same words. Teaching a course the same way again and again for me is a form of suffering. Originally, I was reluctant to give this talk, because there were already tapes. He didn't want to go look for them and listen to them. And again he asked me, and I'm still going to be repeating the same thing. Well, maybe this time it will be more detailed!

So how should we approach this issue of life and death? Should we start from rebirth or from death? I decided to work backwards and start with the exit, death. Then we will look at how people are born into this world, and then talk about life and death—not life, life and death. From the standpoint of logic, these are two different concepts. The topic of life is different from the topic of life and death. The topic of life is huge, it encompasses all life in the universe and includes the issue of life and death within it.

Now, when we talk about life and death, first, we must limit the scope and only talk about the average life and death of humans. There are many people who experience unnatural deaths, accidental deaths. Why is it that some people die unnaturally? Within Buddhist theory, it was that person's karma; and normal death is also one's personal karma.

I have many old friends. People my age, in the nineties, often receive news of the death of old friends. A friend calls to let me know that so-and-so is gone, I dare not say, "Oh that's good!" I would be embarrassed to say this. Sometimes people call and ask: Teacher, are you doing okay? I say, "I'm not dead yet, I can still answer your call!" "Of course! It's good to hear your voice!" People in their 80s and 90s might die at any time. There is nothing good or bad about this.

Recently many old friends have died. I was chatting with one old friend about how, in old times, notifications would be sent out that so-and-so "passed away in his/her bed." When we spoke of someone else's father having passed away, we used formal language saying, "the patriarch was a good person and passed away in his bed." If, at the end of one's life, one passes away in one's own bed, in one's own house, that one had slept in one's whole life, this was considered a normal death. In ancient times, most Chinese built houses around courtyards. The main room was for the elders to sleep, and the children slept in the side rooms. Next to the main room of the elders was the middle hall. When an elder died, the door panel was taken down and the body placed on the door panel in the middle of the middle hall. It was displayed there for three days.

Before being moved to the middle hall, the person needed to be dressed while his or her body was still soft. In ancient times, so-called wealthy families had to prepare six or seven layers of clothes for the dead. As well, each son-in-law had to prepare one quilt, and if there were ten son-in-laws, there would be ten quilts. How were the seven layers of clothes put on? First, the deceased's son stood in the hall and, one by one, put on and then took off each of the seven layers of clothing himself. After taking off a layer, they would lift the corpse up and put it on the deceased. These seven layers of clothing had to be put on while the body was still pliable. After this the body was displayed in the main hall and there were constantly people around to guard it. Why did they need to guard the deceased? Sometimes people have a kind of pseudo-death and come back to life in three or four days. There were many cases of this kind. Therefore, according to ancient Chinese ritual, the body cannot be put in a freezer at the funeral home immediately after one dies. For three days, people "guarded the soul" day and night.

Speaking of this, there is something else you should know about "guarding the soul." In the past, in rural houses, there were always cats and mice running around. The body of the deceased was laying there out in the open. If a cat or mouse ran across the body, the corpse would sit up. Scientifically speaking, it has to do with electro-magnetic induction. Another reason for "guarding the soul" was to keep cats or mice away from the body.

After being on display for three or four days, the person's face and body were covered with cloth and they were put into a coffin. When a person was dying, before they passed away, they were bathed. If it was an old lady, her daughter or daughter-in-law would wash and wipe her body clean and an old man would be washed by his son or son-in-law. There are many details to the ancient customs and ceremonies, this is what was meant by "passing away in one's own bed."

I often say, the higher one's status, the richer the person and the less able to pass away in one's own bed. The person is clearly dying but still gets sent to the hospital and put on life-support. The body may be dead, but the brain cells are still active, the life-support system makes the brain cells die more slowly. The life-support system was originally intended to save a person's life, but now it has become a habit. Many patients are put on life-support as soon as they enter the hospital. In the end, no family members or friends dare to say turn off the life-support and let him go. The result is that the patient suffers. Sometimes this can drag on for a year or two, the dying person is suspended in a vegetable state. The family spends a ton of money, even to the point of ruin. This is why I say that people's karma is really bad now!

It is difficult to die peacefully in your own bed. Now the end is at the hospital, not at home. When you die in the hospital, as soon as your breath stops, you get sent to the refrigerator room. A car from the funeral home comes to pick up your body, and immediately puts you into ice storage. Ice storage is not as bad as being stripped of all your clothes and being put, men, women, and children all together, into the chemical preservative pool to soak like the dead fish. All the corpses floating in the chemical potion. I went in to look and was hit with the fumes of that intensely unpleasant odor! Before the funeral, the body gets fished out of this pond and rinsed with water. Next they put on makeup and clothes, and the person seems to look perfectly normal! In reality, it is like a form of punishment. It's just like when we go buy those small fish or shrimp that have been soaked in some solution...what a circus. Life, what's the point?! It really makes no sense!

There was a situation with a friend of mine who was a Taiwanese legislator, similar to a CPPCC member or a deputy of the People's Congress in the Mainland. He was a great scholar, who insisted on calling me Teacher. Then I, being called Teacher, start to develop a familial feeling, very warm. Well, one night, his wife died. He was away and their children were in America.

After hours of trying to figure out who to get in touch with, a doctor from the hospital eventually got in touch with me and asked me to come identify the body and sign the official papers for him. I often get dragged into such things by others. I had no other choice but to go. It was at night when I arrived at the hospital. I asked where she was and got sent to the morgue. I walked into the morgue, ooh-la-la! Dozens of men, women and children lined up along the upper and lower shelves. Then I saw the person who was in charge of the morgue. It was winter and he was cooking hot-pot. The hot-pot was full of big pieces of meat, and he was sitting there eating it with a bowl of rice. I asked where Mrs. so-and-so was. He pointed, still eating, "over there, go take a look." It's really amazing that this man can sit amidst all those corpses, and that smell, and eat a hot-pot full of meat! Standing next to a body, I asked if this was her. There was a cloth covering her face and I didn't think it was right to uncover her. He said "I'll come," put down his chopsticks, came over and pulled back the cover. "Is that her?" I said, yes, yes, and he asked me to sign something. Oh my, I really had a lot of thoughts and feelings in my heart...

From the end of life to the end of the year—I am reminded of the five blessings that people would write and hang on the door on New Year. The five blessings are "Longevity, prosperity, health, good virtue, and life's final exam." (from the book *Shang Shu* by Hong Fan) The first blessing is "longevity," and next comes wealth or "prosperity." However, high position or officialdom is not a blessing. There is no "status" among the five blessings. The last is "life's final exam." What is this exam? In ancient books, it says "the exam is old age." It means being old is the test. Seventy years is considered old. So then, what do the books say about old age? "Old age is the exam." I often see these kinds of explanations in Chinese, and it ticks me off. They say nothing! "Life's final exam" means to have a good ending, to die well. It's very hard to die well! Longevity is already good enough, but you still need to have a pleasant ending. Therefore, according to ancient Chinese custom, when people over 80 years old pass away, white cloth is not used. Rather, red elegiac couplets and red tents are used because it is seen as a happy event. Why is this? Because they have been blessed with longevity and a good death.

In today's world, it is nearly impossible to pass away in one's own bed. At best, we can die without disease. A few friends' elders passed away like this: they were talking and laughing with their family during dinner. After dinner they said they were tired, so they closed their eyes, leaned back against the chair and departed! My mother was 100 years old when she left. Su-Mei and Chuan-Hong were there. It was New Year's Eve and there was a full house. All the children and grandchildren were there for dinner. She ate two bowls of rice, and then said "I am going to bed." The next day, on the morning of the first day of the first lunar month, my wife found her resting in peace! It's best to leave like this, no illness, just go.

Therefore, Buddhism talks about the impermanence of life and the realm of life. There are four points of view: "Whatever gathers will dissipate; Whatever rises will fall; Wherever there is union, there will be separation; And wherever there is life, there will be death." "Whatever gathers will dissipate." Someone born in poverty might work very hard their whole life to make money. This money will eventually dissipate no matter how much wealth was accrued. In many wealthy families, after the death of the patriarch, the children and wives battle in court over the money and property, leaving behind a trail of infamy and ridicule. "Whatever rises will fall." That which is seen as having a high status, will definitely become low, and those who come to power will eventually lose that power. "Wherever there is union, there will be separation." We are all together now, but one day we will all be scattered. "And wherever there is life, there will be death." This life is completed with death in the end.

Why does Buddhism talk about impermanence? Because there is nothing eternal in the world. Human desire is forever wishing for eternity, wishing to live forever. That is eternally impossible, a foolish wish made by people who cannot see clearly. So the Buddha tells you that whatever gathers will dissipate and whatever rises will fall. Wherever there is union, there will be separation. And, wherever there is life, there will be death. Impermanence is a certainty and a major principle.

So, we must first understand that our human life is a combination of two things, one is the mind or spirit, and the other is the body. The "Book of Changes" talks about yin and yang in tandem. The elements of this body were categorized very clearly by Buddha Shakyamuni 25,600 years ago. The four great elements of the physical world are: earth, water, fire, and wind. In fact, there are five elements including empty space, but empty space need not be mentioned as it must exist. Also, in Chinese we talk about the five elements: metal, wood, water, fire, and earth.

The four great elements are representative of four major functions. They do not refer to specific substances, but represent many, many functions. The various specific phenomena are manifestations of the four major functions. In the same way, the "five elements" are also representative of five types of functions, and it does not refer to a specific material phenomenon. It would be wrong to treat them as specific phenomena. What do the four great elements represent? The great element of earth represents solidity and shape. The great element of water represents wetness and liquids. The great element of fire represents hot, warm, or cold temperatures. The great element of wind represents movement, action, and operation. The energy of airflows and electric currents belong to the phenomenon of wind, and the heat of electric current belongs to the phenomenon of fire.

In terms of natural phenomena, in addition to the earth, water, fire, wind, and space in the physical world, the movement of sound, light, electricity, and chemical transformation are all phenomena caused by the changes of earth, water, fire, and wind. The great elements in the human body are bones, muscles, nerves, and blood, body fluids, endocrine system, body temperature, and the functioning of all organs. Then, scientific research has derived modern physics, chemistry, medicine, pharmacy, geography, physiology, including acoustics, optics, electricity, mechanics, chemistry, and so on.

Just now I said that life is made up of two things. I talked about the body earlier. As for our spirit and thoughts, this part does not belong to the four great elements, but it's functions match the four great elements. In other words, the body of the four great elements is the material world, while the spirit and emotional thoughts are the mental world. When the two meld together and become one, there is this life.

As for how we enter the womb, and everything up to the birth of a baby, we will talk about later. Now let's talk about the process of death. So where does death begin? I often remind people that to maintain physical health they should pay attention to moving their two legs. If you look at a baby lying on a bed, the main activity takes place in those two legs and the hands do not move much. Because the baby's vitality is full, the legs like to move. Healthy babies hold their hands in a fist with the thumb inside. This is called the fist of protection in Esoteric Buddhism. I also often say that we are born grasping and continue to grasp everything in the world—love, relationships, children, money— until the moment of death when there is no choice but to let go. If you look at the dead, they can't grasp anymore. They have all "awakened" and let go completely, ha! Cannot grasp anymore.

After the child is born, within the first year, "seven sitting, eight climbing, and nine teething." This is an old saying, and everyone in the countryside knows that babies will start sitting at seven months; now some children start earlier. They will start crawling at eight months. At nine months they start teething and speech begins after they are one years old. When a baby turns one year old, this is a very happy event for Chinese people because time for the "Zhuazhou."[3] In the book, <u>Dream of Red Mansion</u>, it talked about Zhuazhou, bringing a one-year-old child to a table where the four treasures of study and various toys have been placed. Now people put out cars, trains,

---

[3] Birthday grab or first grab, where various items representing different life paths are placed together and the one that the baby crawls to and picks up tells about the baby's career or personality

gold/silver/gems, and money. In the "Dream of Red Mansion" it says that Jia Baoyu grabbed a container of lady's rouge. So Jia Baoyu had a lifetime of close relationships with women. In "The Biographies of Eminent Monks," some of them, during their Zhuazhou, definitely grabbed Buddhist scriptures with no interest in anything else while others went for books. Whichever object the child likes is a prediction of his or her life based on habit energy, habit patterns, and personality traits.

At one years old, the fontanelle on the top of a baby's head still has a pulse, and the sixth consciousness has not yet fully developed. There is awareness (the root of consciousness, which is also called the seventh consciousness, or manovijnana, the pre-existent, self-grasping ego), but there is no sixth consciousness (the discriminating consciousness), and not much ability to discriminate. After the fontanelle has completely closed, the baby begins to speak, and the post-natal functioning of the discriminating consciousness begins to function.

You see, babies like to move their legs. When they get a bit bigger, they like to run around. Dogs hate them when they are seven or eight years old. If that dog is sleeping, the kids will run over and kick him because their legs love to move. In elementary and middle school, kids love to play sports. By the time you become a boss, middle-aged people like you start to have trouble with legs and you want to put them up. Back in the day, Guanbei

Yang would go to the office, smoke a cigarette, put his legs up on the table, and give orders to people sitting like that. So, is your health in order? It depends on your two legs. When you get old, your legs will be like this when you walk (the teacher imitates an old person hobbling). By checking how flexible your two legs are, you will have a good indication of your physical condition.

Therefore, aging and death begin with the soles of the feet. It used to be said that "cold is born from the soles of the feet." Old people will live longer if the soles of their feet are hot in winter. This is why I often advise you to add clothes, especially women, to wear thicker pants. When we were young, we saw our grandmothers wearing trousers which were gathered at the ankles and so there were fewer gynecological diseases. Now ladies wear bikini briefs and skirts. They want to be beautiful and don't worry about feeling cold. Therefore, there are many gynecological diseases. Cold starts from the soles of the feet and the energetic essence is also born from the soles of the feet. The legs and feet are very important.

I often say, half joking, that you monks chant in the morning and evening prayers, "I go for refuge to the Buddha, the Honored One with Two Legs." The Buddha has two legs, why say "with two legs?" According to the teachings, the two "legs" represent bounteous fortune and wisdom, and so he is called the "Honored One with Two Legs." In this world, generally, wealthy people have no erudition and erudite people have no wealth; there are those who have fortune but no wisdom, and wisdom but no fortune. If a person has wealth, fame, wisdom, and erudition, this is incredible. This person is a respected one with two legs, according to the teachings.

In fact, it is very important to work on the legs and feet! If you are inflexible below the waist and walk stiffly, you are aging. If you can still put your legs up to your head, do yoga easily when you are older, it's fantastic.

Speaking of dying, in fact, we are in the process of dying all the time. We don't just age on a yearly or monthly basis; we are aging hourly, every moment, every second. Zhuangzi put it more succinctly, "As we are born, we begin dying, and as we die, we live." When you are born, you begin to die; that is, life is a process of dying. We are living and dying at all times. Zhuangzi talks about life and one interesting statement of his I often quote is "Do not die waiting for death." This is Zhuangzi's conclusion on the value of life, human life. Look at a person who has lived to a hundred, or one hundred and fifty years old—I myself am ninety years old—they seem alive, but in fact they are just waiting for death.

On the first day you were born, you already started to die. How old did you say this child was? Three years old. Alas, every prior moment of this child is already dead, and throughout all of her days, she will continually die, no matter where or when, continually dwindling and dying. Therefore, when you are born, you will age and you will get sick. Getting old is a kind of syndrome which eventually leads to death. Aging and illness happen in the middle and are a prelude to death. Life and death are relative. From both a relative standpoint and a subjective standpoint, where there is birth, there must be death. It's simply a matter of whether that death comes sooner or later. People wish for some method to stay young and healthy forever, but that is impossible. Although...it is actually kind of possible, however the methods are secret. Some of the secret methods are in the Surangama Sutra, but it depends on how well you can cultivate. Even so, there is no forever, you merely age more slowly.

So now that we have some understanding of this, we'll talk about human death. Previously we talked about people who died peacefully in their own bed. When a person who is ill is about to die, the four great elements undergo major changes. The first to experience obstacles and changes is the great element of earth. The earth element of the human body is the bones and joints. Elderly people and those who have experienced a stroke, lose awareness of half their body. Even some of the muscles, bones, and nerves are already dead; in other words, half of their earth element is already dead. We won't talk about this from a medical perspective now, that gets into much more detail.

Before passing away, one is not able to move one's own body. In Confucian texts, we saw Confucious' student Zengzi, also called Zengcan, who wrote the Great Learning on his deathbed. "On his sick bed, Zengzi called his students and their students to him and said, "Place my hands and my feet properly. The poem says, *'With fear and trepidation, as if standing on the brink of an abyss or walking on thin ice.'* Henceforth, I shall be spared, my little ones!"" Zengzi is dying. Why does he say 'place my hands and my feet properly?' Because he can't move, he asks his students to help him adjust his feet and hands. He is letting them know that he is getting ready to take his last breath and leave. His disciples tell him that his hands and feet have been placed nicely. He said: I tell you now, throughout my entire life, I have been extremely careful. *'With fear and trepidation, as if standing on the brink of an abyss.'* As if I were standing on the edge of a cliff, and just beyond my feet is a ten thousand meter drop into the abyss. If I had accidentally slipped-up, I would incur rancor throughout the ages. It was like walking on thin ice. When the ice has just frozen in early winter, or when it is about to thaw in early spring, you must have skill and competence to walk across; one miscalculation and you will fall through the ice and die. If a person cultivates throughout their entire lifetime and can die with no regret, they can, as Mencius said, "face heaven with no shame, and need not bow to humanity in disgrace." This is truly a great accomplishment.

It is common for people to deceive others, but the strange thing is that people like to deceive themselves. But when someone is about to die, there is no fooling oneself. If you want to end with no need to bow to humanity in disgrace, you must live "as if standing on the brink of an abyss or walking on thin ice." Life is fraught with difficulty, especially when you get tested whether you can be loyal or be a filial child. It all comes down to where your mind is at. If you are afraid that you will lose out, you will fail. Now back to Zengzi: I have lost awareness of my hands and feet, I am half dead. "Henceforth, I shall be spared, my little ones!" At this point, I dare to brag a little and say: I won't be making any mistakes. "My little ones," means you young people should pay attention!

When you begin to lose control of your body, sometimes even turning over can be very difficult. This is the first stage of death, the earth element begins dying. At this point, the person could still be saved through medical intervention.

In the second stage, the great element of water begins to disperse. This is the point when one is really in the process of dying. Looking at their eyes, both pupils are dilated. Although you are right in front of him, to him you seem far away, like a shadow. When you speak to him in a loud voice, it sounds to him like a mosquito—Huh? What? Can't hear you! He will break out in a sticky, cold sweat all over his body. This is the great element of water dispersing. Seventy percent of our body is water and when the water element dissipates, this kind of sweat is released. With the appearance of this phenomenon, there is almost no way to save the person. The moment of death is near. Next, the anus will open and there is a final emptying of the bowels. As well, there is a final release of seminal fluid and a very short moment of sexual pleasure. There is no saving the person at this point. These are the phenomena of the lower half of the body.

Returning to the upper half of the body, starting here in the throat, ahrgh... ahrgh..., breathing becomes very difficult. After the dissolution of the water element, the great element of wind begins to dissipate. The body's Qi (chi energy) rapidly declines, and the person is not able to speak because they lack Qi. At this point the doctor will try to clear the throat and trachea by inserting a tube to clear the phlegm. The water element has stopped flowing and has become sputum. The doctor has to extract the phlegm. The lungs are severely inflamed and the bronchi become blocked by phlegm. After extracting phlegm, the Qi of breath can rise up little by little, and you will hear "er...er...er..." Finally, the breath reaches the Adam's apple, "er...er...," but if it cannot pass beyond there, the person will die.

Long ago, when old friends were passing away, I would ask

the son: Is there a grass lamp? Now people use electric lights, and there are no more grass lamps. Next I'd ask him to bring a chicken feather and rest the feather on the mouth and nose to see if it moves, or use thin paper for the test. If it doesn't move, there's no breathing, and the person has left.

To review, when a person is about to die, they feel like they are being pressed down and not able to move. This is the earth element beginning to die. People who are dying feel like they are in a dream. Some feel like they are in a place which is very dark and others are in a brighter place. There is a feeling of being pressed by something. It is more agonizing than being pressed down in a dream. The experience in a dream is just uncomfortable but at the time of death, it can seem as if two mountains are sandwiching you.

When the great element of water is starting to dissipate, consciousness starts to scatter, as if entering a dream state. It's as if one is under water, or under the ocean. You hear sounds the way you would underwater and you hear the sounds of under the ocean. These sounds are actually changes inside of the body.

When the great element of wind is starting to dissipate, Qi gets stuck in the throat, and the person becomes muddled. Internally, one feels like a typhoon is blowing and it is cold, freezing even. Finally, with a gasp, breath stops.

The death of the great element of wind proceeds step by step, and at the same time, it is connected to the death of the great element of fire. The fire element dissipates as the wind element dies, and body temperature becomes progressively colder. As the last breath comes to a stop in the upper throat, the whole body becomes cold.

Buddhism informs us that this is the time we can test where the dying person will be reborn. If this person has been virtuous and moral throughout their life, they will have a good rebirth. If all of the body has become cold and the chest still remains warm, if the middle of the chest is the last place of the body to retain heat, it means the person will be reborn in the human realm. Of course, this person is still within samsara. Such people, before dying, are clear and alert and have put all of their affairs into order. As well, at the time of death, the person's face looks benevolent and auspicious. This harbinger of the karmic reward of "returning among the people" has already appeared.

If just after death, every part of the body is cold except for the forehead, face, or eyes. If these areas are still warm and are the last to become cold, the person might ascend to heaven. But there are differences, some people's faces look very angry, and they will become asuras. Asuras are also part of the heavenly realms, and are considered a good rebirth. Ascending to this heaven, some become gentlemen, but they have a temper.

Rebirth in either the heavenly realms or as an Asura are both the result of much good merit, but those who become Asuras have a strong habit of killing, have a bad temper, or are aggressive. "I'm going to beat you, you damn..!" That is Asura. Those heading to the heavens are kind and compassionate.

If the whole body is cold but the top of the head is still warm, this person will surely ascend to the Heavens. If the person studied Buddhism, they will have a very good rebirth. If the person practiced well, they might see Amitabha and go to the Pureland of Bliss, or Guanyin Bodhisattva may come to guide them.

These are called the three higher paths going upward. Why is it considered going up? There are two sentences in the Shurangama Sutra: "Purely meditative sends you flying" and "Purely emotional brings you downward." Those who take up spiritual practice, who cultivate themselves, who learn Buddhism, will rise in spirit. "Purely emotional brings you downward." Wallowing in emotions and doing bad things, sends you downward. You will fall into the three lower realms.

The lower three realms are those of hungry ghosts, beasts, and hell. If the whole body becomes cold and the knees are the last place to become cool, this person will be reborn in the animal realm. If the whole body cools down and the lower abdomen still retains warmth, the person is turning into a hungry ghost. Finally, if the whole body goes cold starting from the top going downward, down toward the sole of the foot, if the middle of the sole of the foot is the last place to remain warm, this person is heading to the hell realms. The "death face" of those heading to the three lower rebirths will undoubtedly be very ugly. There is almost no way to test, no chance to touch the body of the person. Especially for modern people, there is virtually no possibility! However, for those who have done well and are headed for rebirth in the three upper realms, it is much easier to check the body warmth.

What about the case when a person dies in a coma, in a state of complete unawareness? In the "Yogacarabhumi Sastra," Maitreya Bodhisattva explains five specific kinds of no-mind, called the "five grounds of no-mind": 1) deep, dreamless sleep no-mind state 2) the unmitigated state of unconsciousness or coma no-mind state 3) the dhyana of no-thought no-mind state 4) the dhyana heaven of no-thought no-mind state 5) *nirodha samāpatti* (the cessation of perception, feelings and consciousness samadhi) no-mind state. Do you all still remember? This mind refers to the sixth consciousness, not to the seventh consciousness (Manas Vijnana) or the eighth consciousness (Alaya Vijnana). It is the seeing, hearing, feeling and knowing functions of consciousness. "Knowing" is the function of the sixth consciousness. "Seeing" is the function of eye consciousness, "hearing" is the function of ear consciousness, and "feeling" is the function of nose, tongue, and body consciousnesses. In the no-mind state, the sixth consciousness has completely shut down and is not functioning.

The first type is "deep, dreamless sleep no-mind state." Deep sleep is being truly asleep; it is a no-mind state. You have to know that it is wrong to say that a person has slept for six hours or ten hours. The person has only truly been completely 'asleep' for fifteen minutes, at most half an hour, and spent the rest of the time dreaming. If you feel that you didn't dream, it's because when you wake up, you forget. In fact, your mind was not at rest. If you can sit in meditation with no thoughts at all, without being groggy, for just fifteen minutes, you can spend the next ten hours doing things and you will be full of energy. Real sleep is a no-mind state, with no thinking. If you are dreaming, you are still thinking.

The second type, "unmitigated state of unconsciousness or coma no-mind state", is to pass out. Some examples of this are when someone gets hit on the head, gets a concussion, and passes out; or receives full anesthesia for surgery; or having a near-death experience. Two of our friends here said that they had died. In fact, they did not really die, but this can also be used as a reference.

The third type is the "dhyana of no-thought no-mind state." One who has achieved the dhyana of no-thought has cultivated the ability to truly stop thinking during meditation. If a person is able to cultivate the dhyana of no-thought, that is an incredible achievement and it is also the ground of no-mind.

The fourth type is the "dhyana heaven of no-thought no-mind state." The future result of cultivating the dhyana of no-thought is rebirth in the Form Realm heaven of no-thought dhyana which is a very high heaven. The heaven of no-thought is one of the four dhyana heavens, the one in which the beings have stopped all thought. Of course they have not become Buddhas or even Arhats. This is a state of concentration, which can also be said to belong to the non-buddhist 'outside paths'. However, being able to cultivate to the point of no-thought is really incredible, and most people cannot achieve this.

The fifth type is "*nirodha samāpatti* (the cessation of perception, feelings and consciousness samadhi) no-mind state." *Nirodha samāpatti* is also called the cessation of perception, feelings and consciousness samadhi. The Great Arahants extinguish all thoughts and feelings, and go beyond all mental and physical states. This is called *nirodha samāpatti*, which is the realm of the Great Arahants. They extinguish all thoughts, reasoning, emotions, delusions, and distinctions, as well there are no physical feelings, or any other kinds of feelings. Turning off perceptions and feelings, turning off these functions which usually dominate things, they enter a state of emptiness, which is the Great Arahants' *nirodha samāpatti.*

These are the five states of no-mind, having no thoughts, and no consciousness. This mind refers to the sixth consciousness, not Manas vijnana or Alaya-vijnana. These five types of no-mind do not include the two no-mind states during birth and death.

Just now I talked about the normal death of ordinary people, the moment they die, they also enter a state of no-mind. Generally, for people who have not practiced spiritual cultivation, how long does the no-mind state of death last? Let's talk about it after dinner.

Session Three

Master Nan: Before dinner, we talked about life and death. When a person is no longer breathing and is completely dead, their sixth consciousness slips into a completely unconscious state. In other words, this unconscious state is like the state of deep sleep at night. It is a state of no-mind, and the sixth consciousness will not function.

Let's diverge for a moment here to answer another question you wanted to ask. Is it alright to cremate the body? Is this the question?

Hu Songnian: Someone asked me about choosing a place for burial after a person dies. According to Chinese customs, there is the theory of Feng Shui, which relates to the fortune of future generations. I don't know how much there is truth behind this. If there is, in the case of cremation does the person also need to be buried in accordance with Feng Shui principles?

Master Nan: This goes to show that students studying Buddhism in the United States, not only the United States, everywhere, in China as well, have the concern that the dead should be buried in a good place from the perspective of Feng Shui because it will affect future generations.

This is a big, complex topic. Regarding the handling of corpses, there are many different customs all over the world. We in China, parts of India, and the Arabs, place importance on burying the dead. There are many types of burial. In the past, Chinese attached great importance to the burial of parents and how that would affect one's life. After death, people were buried by their children and grandchildren. Before the stage of Qin Shihuang and the Han Dynasty, that is, prior to two thousand four hundred and five hundred years ago, there was no such emphasis on Feng Shui as there is now. However, in ancient books it said they emphasized something called "burial divination". Burial places were chosen by divination using the I-Ching hexagrams. Sometimes in serious cases, the emperor personally divined the hexagram to decide whether a burial location was good.

Chinese Confucians placed great importance on harmonious burials. Confucianism values life. Before and after the Spring and Autumn Period and Warring States period, Confucians paid great attention to the health and death of elders. After death, for the sake of filial piety, children and grandchildren must choose a good place so that the deceased will have a peaceful residence. It was not for the sake of blessing future generations with wealth and status. In ancient times, it was merely in the spirit of filial piety and affection for one's elders that one would find a good place to bury them and safeguard their bodies.

After the Eastern Han Dynasty, from the beginning of the

Wei and Jin Dynasties, Chinese liked to choose good locations for burial and not use divination. This site selection required an understanding of geographic feng shui, what would now be known as underground environmental selection. The belief was that it would have a bearing on the quality of future generations. This kind of knowledge only became popular after the Jin Dynasty. To choose the right topography, the geographical situation and environment need to be taken into account. In addition to topography, Qi, Yin-Yang and Five Elements Feng Shui, horoscopes, etc. also must be calculated. It has been passed down to the present, and it is believed that the tomb will affect future generations. The Chinese people are heavily influenced by this, they still can't get out of this concept.

Do the ancestor's bones really affect future generations? This can be called a superstition, it's not reasonable. People from other places, other ethnic groups throughout the world don't use Feng Shui burials and their offspring live good lives and thrive!

The Muslim funeral rites of the Arabs also includes ground burial, but they are different from ours. In China, Confucianists put the most emphasis on funerals. They have four key words, "clothes, cloth, coffin, and cover." 'Clothes' are to be put on the deceased and the 'cloth' is for putting all around the body. Once the coffin has been arranged, there is still an ornate outer covering for the coffin. In addition to all this, there is also the tomb, added together, it cost a lot of money. During the Spring and Autumn Period and Warring States Period, Confucian customs were like this.

"Clothes, cloth, coffin, and cover" was a lavish burial, but there were many people who opposed this. Taoists opposed this and Mozi, who was a contemporary of Confucius, absolutely opposed it. Mozi followers advocated frugal burials. Confucius also stated in the Book of Changes, *I Ching*, that, in ancient times [ancient times from Confucius' perspective] the custom when looking for a place to bury a person who died, was "no seal and no tree." 'No seal' does not mean not sealing the coffin, but not decreeing a specific plot of land to be used for graves. You simply use land belonging to your own family. 'No tree' means no grave markers, no monuments, and no trees, nothing should be used to designate the site.

People in later generations valued 'clothes, cloth, coffin, and cover' and emphasized filial piety. After one's parents died, this kind of lavish burial insisted upon by Confucians showed the weight of one's loss. Taoists laughed at this, death is a natural thing. "People are born to live their lives, and then die and return back." Dying is like going home. Do whatever you want after death. Don't pay attention to this form. Just pack him up and bury him. As for the Mohist school, Mozi's faction had a great influence. They opposed thick burials and advocated thin burials. They were simple and clear, and the burial was just fine, and they did not care about the offspring. The influence of feng shui on the offspring was a thought added by later generations.

Muslim funerals are also very simple. They have a taboo against using the word "dead", because Islam regards passing away as finally returning to the place they belong. Their understanding is that with the disappearance of "Galabu" (physical body), the "Rohan" (the spirit) becomes elevated. It is the return of life, not the end of life. They call death "Impermanence" or "Mao Ti", or "Returning to Truth". "Mao Ti" is Persian, which means death; "Returning to Truth" is reserved for the death of religious people. There is an Muslim saying, "A Muslim can return to the land anywhere under the sky." It advocates that "being placed in the ground, one can rest in peace." Muslim people should be buried wherever they meet with their 'impermanence.' There is no need to be returned home to be buried. It also advocates that "within three days the burial must take place." Generally, if the 'impermanence' occurs in the morning, the burial takes place in the afternoon and if the 'impermanence' happens in the evening, the burial takes place on the morning of the next day. It cannot exceed three days. The corpse is scrubbed clean, wrapped in white cloth, put in the coffin, and carried to the dug grave. Pulling out the movable board under the coffin, the corpse falls into the grave facing the direction of the holy land of Mecca. Finally they fill the hole with clumps of earth and bring the empty coffin back. Muslims forbid cremation, they specify land burial after 'impermanence'. They do not set up an altar for the deceased, do not give flower wreaths and couplets, and do not entertain during the funeral. The funeral ceremony is simple and quiet. There is no motorcade, no hired drummers, trumpeters, or performers. It is all done without pomp. There is no need for burial objects, no paper carts, horses, virgins, etc. No sacrifices are allowed during the funeral, and no memorial services are held. This is equivalent to the frugal burial that Mozi encouraged, so simple. The body is made of earth, water, fire and wind. Dust to dust, the body returns to the earth.

Other ethnic groups have other types of burials. In Tibet, sky burials are prevalent. Once a date is chosen, the master who specializes in sky burials performs the ceremony. The corpse is dissected and the pieces are placed around the burial area for the birds to eat. An offering is made for all living beings, and the body returns to nature.

In some places, such as Southeast Asia, there is a custom of water burial, where the body is placed in water and allowed to float away. Some Western countries also have water funerals, where the corpses are placed in special boats, sometimes covered in flowers, and set adrift.

Therefore, earth, water, fire, and wind are all able to expunge a corpse. When buried in the earth, it will naturally become soil. It can even be eroded away by the wind.

Cremation was advocated by the Buddha. "One fire can burn away past, present and future karma." One fire burns this body. This body is a composite of past, present and future cause and effect, and the fire is used to cleanse it.

In Buddhism, karma is divided into three categories: good, bad, and neutral karma. The "karma" in the saying that "one fire can burn past, present and future karma" does not include "evil" karma, "evil" meaning completely evil. There are only three types of behavior we engage in during our lifetime. Sometimes we do good deeds where both thoughts and actions are good and sometimes what we do is bad. Lastly, there are things we do unintentionally, mindlessly, or without any conscious thought of doing something good or bad. This is neutral karma. For example, when you are asleep at night and a mosquito bites you, you unwittingly smack it, and then go back to sleep again. It's only when you get up in the morning and see the blood stains that you are aware of having killed a mosquito! This is not a deliberate killing, it is a neutral karma of killing. According to the law, there was no motivation to kill. Another example is if we were sitting here carving something and the knife accidentally went flying. If, as a result, we wounded someone downstairs, this is also considered neutral karma.

People call it the fire that can burn past, present, and future karma, but it can only burn the karma of the appearance of this physical shell. This body is only a very small part of one's past, present, and future karma. Don't think that "one fire" can burn away all of your past, present, and future karma and you won't need to pay back any karmic debts. Of course you have to pay them back, karma cannot be burned. This is a principle of the Consciousness Only School. The Alaya Consciousness keeps all the seeds of your actions, and recompense or retribution will happen when the time comes. All the actions of body, speech and mind are recorded in the Alaya Consciousness and become seeds. When a karmic seed is mature, it becomes a functioning karmic result. The body is only a very miniscule part of the functions and phenomena of the Alaya Consciousness, and only a very small part of one's past, present, and future karma, just a tiny phenomenon. Now we are talking about the physical body, so pay special attention! "One fire can burn past, present, and future karma" is talking about the body, not the Consciousnesses.

If we say that a tomb will affect the success of future generations, this is reasoning, just talk. It can also be said that this reasoning is a product of human concepts. Conceptually, it is believed that Feng Shui will affect future generations. If you made a statistical analysis of the people throughout the whole country of people whose ancestors' burial site did not have good Feng Shui but were successful and of those whose ancestors had good burial sites but were unsuccessful, you would know the truth. We just mentioned that this is a product of reasoning believed by the average person, and backed by a set of conceptual theories which seem to add further confirmation, but it is actually unreasonable.

What is good Feng Shui? If the burial ground does not flood when it rains and is not plagued by strange winds, the Feng Shui is good. This is the spirit of filial piety. For example, sitting here you make sure that the window behind me is closed so the wind doesn't blow on me. Both wind or rain can be harmful, so I remind people to put on more clothes, cover their knees, and keep warm. That's the reasoning behind it. Nowadays, cremation is encouraged, so there is no need to find a good burial place to show filial piety.

So you ask, will burial in a good feng shui place have any big impact on future generations? The answer is no. According to Buddhist principles, all of the bones and remains of our ancestors, our descendants, the ancestors of friends, all the remains are merely a phenomenal expression of their essence, their 'life function'. This life function is called the Alaya Consciousness. The physical body and the Alaya are of the same essence and each person's is a result of their own individual karma. It's not that if I am good, he is not good, and if he is good, I am not good. This is not reasonable. There are a lot of principles which can be taught here. To use a sentence in the Shurangama Sutra, "do not interpret it as holy," just don't take it as being some kind of exalted truth.

If you say you want to find a good place for your parents' burial to make you feel at ease, this is right; this is the spirit of filial piety. If you chose the burial spot which will be good for yourself and your offspring, this would be wrong. If you "interpret it as holy," believing in such a theory, then, you are being "influenced by demons." It's just craziness. Those are demon ideas, not the truth.

Okay, I have covered this issue.

Before eating, we were at the point when someone died and was still laying there. The great elements of earth, water, fire and wind had dispersed. Let me add that if a person dies normally, which of the four great elements goes awry first? The earth element scatters, right? Which is second ? The water element disperses. Thirdly, wind and fire disperse together, as they have come together.

In relation to this point, those of you who study Buddhism should pay special attention. We are alive now and are able to think. Where does this mind, this consciousness come from? The Consciousness Only School, the Dharmalaksana teachings point out the three conditions of life: warmth, lifeforce, and consciousness.

Warmth refers to the temperature needed to keep the body alive. This warmth or temperature is related to the great element of fire. Warmth is required for the presence of the lifeforce. That is why, on our planet, the temperate and tropical places are biologically lush and abundant. In the cold zones, this is not the case. There is a much smaller range of biological species. Warmth and lifeforce are necessary conditions for the conscious mind to function. Warmth, lifeforce and consciousness are a trinity.

So what is the relationship between the warmth, lifeforce, and consciousness and the great element of wind which we call Qi/Chi (including innate, prenatal Qi/Chi). What is their relationship? The function of Qi/Chi is the bedrock of life, it is the foundation for warmth and consciousness. They rely on the functioning of Qi, rely on the great element of wind, not only postnatal breathing, but also prenatal innate Qi. So when a person dies, when the last breath stops, their wind has stopped functioning. The functioning has stopped! It's not that the wind element no longer exists, the wind element is still there, but the coming and going, the arising and ceasing of the breath, the functioning, has stopped. The coming and going of the breath is life and death. Following this, the great element of fire stops working, and this is called the death of the person. After the person dies, the body becomes cold.

When someone is alive and you pick them up, man, woman, parent, sibling...you can pick them up, even carry them on your back, and they feel buoyant. When the person's Qi is no longer there, s/he will feel very heavy and is hard to pick up. Therefore, when we are alive, our bodies feel light and flexible, and move agily, which is the function of Qi. When people get older, the body starts to feel heavy and clumsy, even rigid, because the Qi is already weak. The water element increases greatly, and this imbalance of water causes illness as the strength of fire decreases. Now people joke that the "thief" is already half dead. Nothing works anymore.

Here is a scientific question. The body cools down and dies. So, at temperatures below zero, is there any 'warmth'? If you give a scientific answer, it should be said that there is still 'warmth', but it is a 'warmth' of some degrees below zero. To us this is very icy, but it cannot be said that this is not the element of fire.

Earth, water, fire and wind are the four great elements. Each of them contains the functions of all four elements. For example, the element of fire also contains the elements of water, wind, earth, and space. Each one is like this. These functions are all contained in the original nature. At the same time, Buddhism tells you very scientifically that the four elements each has its own specific nature, the four great elements of earth, water, fire and wind, each has its own range of physical properties, but there is no self-nature. Each of the four has its own range and established identity. For example, if there is a fire burning and it grows big, when you pour water on it, if the water power is stronger than the fire, the fire will be extinguished. The water overpowers the fire. If the firepower is higher than the water power, the water will boil and dry up. Therefore, the four elements each has its own specific nature, but no self-nature. They all have separate functions, and each has its own scope of action. However, their functions can both strengthen each other or destroy each other. If one has more strength, it will overpower the others with less. These principles sound very simple to everyone, but if you look into these from a scientific perspective, it is highly complex.

Therefore, the "four elements have different natures" is very scientific. The four great elements are four categories of functions and phenomena. There is no independent self. It can also be said that their self-nature is emptiness and selflessness. They are all the function of the original nature, and arise together in the unity of mind and matter. So the changing phenomena of the four elements, from birth to death to dissolution—these changes are quantitative and qualitative, and the qualitative and quantitative changes mutually influence each other.

The four great elements, and in addition great emptiness, great awareness, and great consciousness, these seven functions have no life or death, no increase or decrease, they are all the functions of the original nature, having no independent self existence. What is meant by having no self? There is no real independent existence. For example, the various organs of our body, the heart, liver, spleen, lungs and kidneys have their own functions, but each organ is not really independent. Although the functions are different, they all belong to this body. Upon leaving the body, the form and function of existence changes.

The nature of the seven great elements is the same nature and principles of our lives. They are neither born nor perish, neither increase nor decrease. The so-called birth and death, gathering and dispersion, increase and decrease, pure and impure, superior and inferior, good and evil, right and wrong, cause and effect, etc., all material phenomena, spiritual phenomena, and functions of the universe are all the changing appearance and functions of the seven great elements. In the words of the Surangama Sutra, the seven great elements are "pure original nature, ubiquitous throughout the Dharma realm, in accord with the heartminds of all sentient beings, should be known and measured...prefer to have a location, and are discoverable through karma." The seven great elements are inherently not arising or ceasing, not pure or impure, not increasing or decreasing. They are all part of the unity of mind and matter of the original nature, of the functioning of the original nature. The differences in the wisdom of sentient beings result in differences in individual and group behaviors, the results of which are wide and varied. These actions and results are actually made by sentient beings themselves, there is not someone else in charge.

In regards to earth, water, fire, and wind having no self-nature means that they do not exist independently and do not have their own individual eternal and unchanging nature. They are all functions of the body, just like the limbs of a person have their own functions, but they do not exist independently. Whether it be water, fire, or wind, each is in a constant state of changing and returning to emptiness; and this changing is because of emptiness. This is all physical science. It is the deepest relationship between qualitative change and quantitative change, and now natural science research is also advancing in this direction. Our friend, President Zhu of the University of Science and Technology, is writing about this in a book on quantum mechanics for a general audience which is completely scientific. He sent me the manuscript, and in reading it, I admire him very much.

Let's bring our attention back to our dead person who is still lying there! We were following the process of dying up to the moment of death, and at this time the person is completely dead. I was saying that I wanted to add that before dying, the earth element changes drastically. People start to age, and cannot move their body well anymore. They feel stiff. All of you are not young anymore. I can see that, just like me, you are all getting to be very old, and your body is not as flexible as when you were young. But as for you, you think you still have a thousand years to live, but you don't realize that you are already aging. This is very distressing, such low wisdom and thinking. Compare yourself with when you were a teenager. I sometimes test myself, to see if I can do all the movements I did when I was a teenager and I can. Why? Because I focus on practicing them and exercising. You don't pay attention to these things, so no matter if it's how you walk, your eyes or anything, you seem very old. I think back to when I was a teenager, if I came face to face with people your age, I would have run away. I couldn't stand being with the living dead, those old ladies and old men! Aye, but now, you are very lively bunch and still feel that you have a boundless future. Sometimes I think it's funny, hehe, foolish rascals! Hahaha, the Buddha said, "foolish sentient beings," stupid and foolish. Foolish means lacking wisdom.

Now as people age, the discriminating sixth consciousness becomes more and more obstinate, and the elderly become more and more annoyingly unobjective. This creates a generation gap between the old and the young, and they cannot agree on things. As soon as an old person opens his or her mouth, they start to find fault with the youth saying, "I have been around for how many years now? I think I know better than you!" But in fact, this is not reasonable. These are stupid and foolish elderly sentient beings. Having lived for dozens of years, the sixth consciousness has become very polluted and not having had much wisdom to begin with, it usually declines with age. All you have is just a little more experience. In terms of manifesting inherent wisdom, relying on experience often becomes an obstacle and a pollutant. The wisdom of young people, especially children, does not rely on acquired knowledge or experience. That wisdom is higher than yours! Nevertheless, the elderly tend to be stubborn and critical.

When death has come to the earth and water elements and they have undergone drastic changes, the sixth consciousness slowly dissipates. The person becomes sluggish and muddled, can't control his thoughts, and can't even be bothered to think. When a person gets old, and you try to talk about something new, "Ahh, I don't know, I don't even want to think about it." Old people think about things that happened when they were young. If you tell them about current events, they forget about them straight away. If they read books, they don't remember what they have read. Old people can't study. They read something, it makes sense, but they can't remember a word. The brain is already dead. Therefore, even though you are studying now, you are not as capable as I am at my age. If I want to remember something, I can remember it very deeply, the same as when I was young. You don't want to remember and it is not because you refuse but because much of your consciousness has already died. Don't fool yourself thinking that you are still really alive. The older you get, the more tainted and corrupted the knowledge in your consciousness becomes. The older you get, the more and more troublesome things become. The clarity and wisdom of the mind get covered by layer upon layer of pollution.

Therefore, when you sit in meditation, let go of all your illusions. That is, remove all the colors you have painted, get rid of them layer by layer. When you have cleared all of them, you will restore your original lifeforce. But you can't do it, so when you die, you will just be like ordinary people. When the water element dissipates, the sixth consciousness becomes scattered, and you can't be the master of it. The only one thing still left is 'knowing'. "Oh noooo, my God, I'm dying!" That is the seventh consciousness, the root of consciousness, speaking. The distinguishing consciousness no longer has clarity.

When the last breath, the bedrock of life, when the last breath has been drawn and has dissipated, the fire element is gone. After this, the seventh consciousness, the root consciousness, completely separates. It is only after this separation that true and actual death has occured. However, the general materialist view is that if a person is dead, there is nothing left.

After death, the four great elements no longer function as living being and the fundamental roots of life have scattered. What about this body? If it is just left here, how does it decompose? This is what is described in the meditation on impurities of the body and the skeleton meditation.

If the body were laying here, we would see that it does not immediately begin to decompose. It doesn't really start visibly decomposing until ten or more hours later. The flesh around the eyes is the first place we see decay. When conducting an autopsy, a forensic examiner first examines the eyes of the corpse to see how long this person has been dead.

After taking the last breath, the body is soft, so this is when people must hurry to dress the deceased. After a few hours, the body stiffens and it is difficult to put on clothes because the joints can no longer move.

About ten hours later, the body begins to gradually soften again as bruises appear on the skin and decay sets in. The four elements slowly disperse. Water returns to water, earth to earth, fire to fire, and wind to wind. After a period of time, all returns to emptiness.

What does the disintegration of the earth, water, and fire elements have to do with us? This is a function of the Eighth Consciousness, the Alayavijnana. What happens if the dead person has been lying there less than twenty hours, and people call monks to come and recite scriptures or recite the Buddha's name next to the body. This is another big topic. I will talk about it later.

Last year, for example, one of our classmates passed away. Everyone rushed there, someone pulled the hair on the top of his head [to indicate where to leave the body from] and told him, "So-and-so, don't hang on, just let go and recite Buddha's name! We will all recite with you," and everyone stood by and helped recite "Namo Amitabha." They led him in passing on and reminded him, "Listen and follow the sound of Buddha chanting, follow the light of the Buddha."

Now that there are good Buddha recitation machines, turn it on as soon as possible. Tell the deceased to listen, and keep reminding them to pay attention to the chanting because they are no longer able to focus their attention at that time. Many people have studied Buddhism for a lifetime. When they are about to die, they can't recite the Buddha's name anymore. They wish to recite but can't. Usually because they have no wisdom, they think they have to recite Namo Amitabha out loud in order to qualify as reciting Buddha's name. This is not right! If you truly recite the Buddha's name or mantra, although you are not able to even recite one word orally, if you still think of Buddha or Zhunti Bodhisattva in your heart, if you have this thought, this is called "reciting the Buddha's name." I want to remind everyone that this thought is called right mindfulness.

The person standing closest reminded him, "Classmate, don't forget the Buddha, leave from here," gently pulling some hairs on the top of his head to remind him. Then told him, "No matter what you see, it's the same as meditating, whatever happens just ignore it. It doesn't matter if you see scary demons, Yama, heavenly beings; don't be afraid of any scary visions and don't be tempted by anything pleasant. Just long for the Buddha with all your heart, that's all..." If he can do this, he will break free from this life's fate, and his fate/karma in the next life will be different.

At this stage, the people next to the deceased can talk all they want, but even before death, speaking in a loud voice sounded like a mosquito buzzing. So at this time, it's better to use clean, pure Sanskrit together with a chime. The sound of the chime will effectively draw the person's attention and then remind him: "Holding the Buddha in your heart, move on. Just like in meditation, do not pay attention to any states which arise, all fears, emotions, sorrows, sorrows, or any other phenomena. They are deceiving and if you pay attention to them, they will trick you into another life. Stay fully focused on the Buddha." While ringing the chime, remind the person and lead him or her to recite the Buddha's name together.

This is why I ask you to practice meditation, ignore all thoughts, feelings, and all states, and to slowly cultivate concentration in walking, standing, sitting and lying. The Diamond Sutra tells you, "All appearances are illusory." Are you able to do this? This is the time when it will be tested. When a person who has really practiced is dying, his or her mind is correctly focused. For example, a person who cultivates Tantric Buddhism, or a person who cultivates Pure Land Buddhism and holds Amitabha Buddha in mind, at this time, will not be able to recite out loud. His or her strength will be lost and consciousness dispersed. This person will not be concerned with whether they will live or die, their entire focus is on holding the image of Buddha in mind. In the case of a Christian, a person like this will be saved and ascend to heaven. This is called taking the Buddha to heart, and not just merely chanting his name.

People who don't understand this will say, "Friend, now is the time to recite the Buddha's name!" Many people who have studied Buddhism have said to me, "Te...Te...Teacher...I can't re...re...cite." I said, "You fool! Aren't you talking to me? If you can talk to me, you can recite! To recite Buddha is to have the idea of a Buddha in your mind, not to recite Amitabha Buddha with your mouth." But at this point, the person can no longer understand because their consciousness lacks strength. So many people who study Buddhism, whether they study Tantra, Zen, or Pure Land Buddhism, in the end, don't have what it takes and cannot be the masters of their fate. Four words are used to criticize this: "uncontrolled death, futile life"(浪死虛生). Even if you were a monk, or a lay Buddhist, or belonged to another religion, if you are not 'at the helm' during your passing, you have lived your life in vain. Therefore, many religious devotees and Buddhists have not benefited from their faith.

Now let's return to the dying process. As we were saying earlier, the person has stopped breathing, has lost consciousness, and has entered a state of mindlessness. During the period of time when the dying person is close to taking their last breath, we can help our dying friend, reminding them and leading him to hold the Buddha in mind. This is both objective and effective.

So, how do people who have actually died give rise to a bardo body? We have just introduced up to the end of this life, death. Before the transformation into the next life, the in-between 'existence' is called the bardo. Chinese people generally call it *'ling huen'* 靈魂 (akin to soul). The bardo body is not ghosthood. Having become a ghost is a new life, a life of a ghost. Although the bardo body is not a ghost, it is more powerful than a ghost. The bardo body has magical powers! When a person has died and begun their bardo existence, they have no space limitations. As soon as you think of your relatives or loved ones in the United States, you will be next to them immediately. You will tell your friends in the United States, "I am dead, don't be sad," but the other person can't hear you. However, those in the bardo can hear everything the living people say. The bardo body has the five supernatural abilities, the magical powers of the gods. The bardo body can go anywhere, through mountains, rivers, walls, time and space, without obstacles. It is faster than the speed of light, so I call this "the speed of thought" which is amazingly fast!

In fact, you people sitting in front of me, you people who are studying Buddhism, are not really practicing at all, not working hard, and don't even understand an iota, including you young people. So you practice meditation. I often tell you to pay attention. You must know that there are many moments between one breath and the next. There are 60 moments in a snap of your fingers. In the length of a moment, there are 960 changes in your consciousness. You will find that your mind is not in a real state of meditation and tranquility. The rapid changes in your thoughts are so fast, you cannot see them. How many times faster than the speed of light, you can't calculate.

You can see this if you achieve samadhi. Throughout the day and night, within 24 hours, 1.3 billion mind-moments spin around. The number is horrifying! Our thoughts change so quickly, like the Monkey King, one somersault lands him thousands of miles away! With the mind jumping around like that, there is never a moment of peace.

One's chaotic thought world will only become clear and pure when one has cultivated samatha and vipassana. What is this change? It is a change of the samskara skandha, a change of action. It is only through this purification that one can enter this state of concentration. You guys think that, this person attained dhyana, that person attained dhyana. Yeah, yeah, attained dhyana...totally fooling yourselves and others! It's a joke, which of you actually attained dhyana? You can't even see when your thoughts are moving. For example, when I talked to XX, I said, don't talk nonsense. He said, "Teacher, I wasn't talking nonsense, I only mentioned a few things," "All nonsense!" "I said this because..." "I have the authority to joke about this, but you don't." Think about it, it's very scary. You are clearly fooling yourselves and you don't even know it!

The mind-moments of the bardo turn very quickly. The bardo body has the five superpowers: the power to go anywhere, the power to see everything, the power to hear everything, the power to know people's thoughts, and the power to know past and future lives. After dying, when a person wakes up, their bardo body is born. Seeing everyone crying, the bardo person is right there telling us not to cry, "I've passed away, I'm very sad too, don't cry!" Pulling everyone and pleading, but nobody hears. The bardo person can hear what we say and see what we do any place, any time. Mountains and rivers and walls are no hindrance, the physical world presents no obstacle whatsoever.

It is hard to tell how long it takes for ordinary people to go from the completely unconscious state of death to the formation of the bardo body. Of course there is a time period. To be precise, it is very difficult to estimate using the current scientific calculation methods. We ordinary people sleep for about five or six hours and six or seven hours before waking up. From complete death to beginning to wake up in the bardo, it takes about ten hours.

Waking up in the bardo body is just like we wake up from sleep. So when you talk about spiritual cultivation, there's a question I would like to ask everyone. You have all been sleeping for decades, how do you wake up? May I ask, who knows how they wake up? I'm afraid no one knows. You may claim that you know but it's impossible. You only know when you recognize it after you have woken up. That's the function of the discriminating consciousness, and that's not what I mean.

In other words, we lay in bed at night and fall asleep. Everyone has fallen asleep for decades. Do you know how you fall asleep? You don't know that either. If you know, this "knowing" obviously means that you are not asleep, right? If you have fallen completely asleep, there is no 'knowing'. Right now I ask you, before your mother became pregnant with you, how did you get here? You do not know. How did you leave after death? You don't know either. The two questions are the same, but the scope is different.

Objectively, being awake is equal to being alive, falling asleep is equal to dying; after waking up, it is another life and death. In terms of life and death, 'life' is not merely being born from our parents, and 'death' is not just when we die. In fact, we go through birth and death every day and night. At a more subtle level, each mind-moment is birth and death, death and birth. And you have no knowledge of this.

From before we ate dinner until now, how many births and deaths of thoughts and concepts have there been? Even within our metabolism, there have been countless births and deaths. Before eating, we all sat there resting, talking and waiting for dinner. After the meal, my good friends got together and asked XX to play around (referring to super powers of seeing that ordinary people don't have). Hey, what do you see? He said he sees this or that, sees this or that about your body, stuff like this.

All this kind of nonsense. Each mind-moment is a life and a death, all pass.

Right now is a mind-moment, every thought is a life and death, but you don't see this clearly. If you don't see clearly into this moment-by-moment birth and death, how can you cultivate? Oh, I'm chanting Buddha! I'm meditating! I'm chanting a mantra! I'm doing visualization! Everyone is deceiving themselves.

Cultivation is learning wisdom. It's not just casual religious belief. Everything I am able to tell you today comes from my wisdom, not from what I read in the Buddhist scriptures. It's all there in the Buddhist scriptures! However, you wouldn't be able to understand. You are listening to me now, and think you understand. What do you actually know for yourself! I understand, you are just listening to me talk about it. You are what are known as 'Hearers'. You heard what I said and think you understand it, but you haven't proven it to yourself. You listened to what I told you, which is my truth. You didn't reach the truth yourself. You haven't proven it to yourself. What's the use of understanding! Don't lie to yourself.

You friends like to come here every night saying: Teacher, I feel better just looking at you. Oh, so you feel 'comfortable' sitting there listening to me showing off! It costs money to go to the teahouse, you have to pay money to go to the dance hall, but here there is tea, you can watch me showboating, you don't spend a dime, of course it's 'comfortable'! Who are you kidding! All deluding yourselves, thinking that you're cultivating, what cultivation?

That's why I often say that you need to understand Master Yongjia's two words when you truly practice: "The true source of reality is to be recognized, it is not created by causes." That is liberation through wisdom, not effort. You first need to understand this truth, you need wisdom to become liberated, blindly practicing doesn't work. Furthermore, practice is a science. Understand this first, then seek verification.

We have been talking for a long time, and our dead guy is still laying there in the no-mind stage of death. The bardo body has not yet arisen. In order to talk about the bardo body, you will immediately discover that there are many related issues that you need to know about first. This is why my talk meandered for a long time.

Now, let's continue with our person's death. When the bardo body arises, it's as if the person suddenly wakes up. At that time, when the deceased person is about to wake up, the Buddhist scriptures tell us that an intense light will come just before, very intense. But you must pay attention to what the Buddhist scriptures say, don't be fooled. This light is not the light of the sun, the moon, or the light of electric lamps, not any kind of external light, but rather, the light of wisdom. It's equivalent to what I was asking you earlier, how do you know that you have woken up? What is the first moment of waking? People don't know, they only recognize the moment after having woken up, that first moment is the light of wisdom. After we wake up from normal sleep, our eyes have not opened yet, and we feel awake. This is already a second thought. The first mind-moment after we have had enough sleep—snap! Similar to, "pop!" the light switch is turned on. This is the light, the light of wisdom; it doesn't have shape or form. But sometimes there are signs, such as when we wake up very early in the morning, or wake up after a noon nap. You are half awake, a little bit confused and there seems to be some light—you have had this experience, right? The light is hazy and dim.

So, after dying one enters into the bardo as if waking up. This stage is called the bardo body existence. The bardo person feels as if they are alive, there's body feeling, can see, can hear, but wait...huh? They are all crying. Oh my god! I am dead! After crying themselves, the person in bardo will pull on their loved ones saying, don't cry, I've passed over, don't be sad. The bardo person not only can hear people close by, but also those crying for them far away in foreign countries, and can be together with them instantly. One moment here with you, the next moment in another country far, far away. The magical powers of bardo existence are really immense.

The bardo body is just like the dream body. Think about it, do you have a body in your dreams? Yes, you do. In the dream, you not only see delicious food, you also smell the aroma. You cry, you laugh, you feel that the fire is hot and the water is cold. If you are cut by a knife, you will bleed and feel pain. The same principle applies to the bardo. The bardo body is like a dream body. If you see something frightening in a dream, you will run away fearing death, right? The same is true of the bardo. Why use the word 'body'? Because it also has the functions of eye consciousness, ear consciousness, nose consciousness, tongue consciousness, body consciousness, mental consciousness, and thought. This body arises from the mind, but it has those functions. In other words, it does not have physical eyes, nose, tongue, ears, brain, or body, but can still sense everything, appearances, sounds, fragrances, tastes, touch, and mental phenomena. This is called the bardo body.

Well, up to now we have only discussed as far as the emergence of the bardo body. But at the beginning today, I told you that the understanding of past, present, and future karma and the six paths of rebirth form the foundation of Buddhism. The Six Paths have many manifestations of life forms. What I have been talking about today is from human existence, specifically a normal life and death, right? I did not talk about the life and death of other life forms, nor about unnatural deaths of people. Everyone needs to remember this. If you don't have this sense of the lecture's logic, don't come and listen to my lectures. Don't mistake or misunderstand what I say. Remember, now we are talking about normal human death.

In fact, it is not easy to have a bardo existence after death. Good people who have done many good things throughout their entire life and who have cultivated spiritually don't go through bardo existence after death. Such people immediately ascend to heaven as soon as they stop breathing. A monk or a layperson who has successfully cultivated will take rebirth in the Sukhavati Pureland, or some other Buddha land. Sometimes the breath is just about to stop and they have already arrived at the Pureland without passing through the bardo, without stopping in the middle. Very bad people immediately become hungry ghosts, beasts, or go to hell. They don't have a bardo existence, they just go straight down. So, it's easy to talk about the bardo body but not to experience it. You still get to hang around for a while.

When I started studying Buddhism, there was a group of senior practitioners of Tantric Buddhism and Chan who loved and cared for me very much. We must have had good karmic connections. I feel I owe them a debt of gratitude. We chatted together, and one senior practitioner asked me: Hey, brother, there are two places that the bardo person cannot go, do you know what they are? I said, I know! Some of them were testing me, some really didn't know. Which two places? One place that you cannot enter is a Bodhimandala, which is a place of enlightenment. For example, when Buddha Shakyamuni was meditating under the Bodhi tree, a bardo person could not enter that realm. If they did, they would also enter into enlightenment and become a Buddha. This also means a meditation hall like the one we are in right now talking about this topic. A bardo person cannot get in either. Except if I said in my mind, all dharma protectors, please let them come in and listen and create a good karmic relationship. Otherwise, a bardo person cannot enter this light of wisdom.

The second place that they cannot enter is the 'birth-gate'. The 'birth-gate' is a woman's birth canal. The place where the child exits from during birth in the lower part of a woman. Why can't the bardo person enter the birth-gate? Oh, I said why are you so stupid! If they enter the birth-gate, they will take rebirth and become a baby. The bardo person cannot enter a Bodhimandala or the birth-gate; if they enter, they are no longer a bardo person. As for all other places, bardo persons are unstoppable.

In fact, these bodies we are living in now, these other intermediary bodies, are similar. What we want to think about, man wants woman, woman wants man, want to imagine making love. You can imagine you are making love, as if it was real but it is not the same. You can't actually do it though, why? This has to do with giving permission.

Is there life and death in the bardo existence? There is life and death, a change of body every seven days. The bardo person loses consciousness, and then wakes up in a new bardo body.

I have watched for decades, as I have lived to this ripe old age. How many storms of the world have passed! I've seen many friends...makes me really sad...I have seen some things, oiyoiyoi! I saw that the person had already become half animal, and didn't know. Some were already halfway to hell, even though they were still alive here. In particular, some butchers who have killed for decades have already started to resemble the animals they kill but don't know it. Many people have already changed before even reaching the bardo. This is karma, cause and effect.

Again, look at what the Buddhist scriptures say in regards to which of the six realms people have come from. There are those who are about to enter one of the terrible realms or those from one of the terrible realms who have just been reborn as a human. It all shows in the person's habits, residual habits, and appearance, but you aren't able to see it. So, what is supernatural power? Wisdom is true supernatural power, and with it you can see where this person came from because there are still residual habits brought over from that life which have not yet been cut off.

A bardo body has a lifespan of seven days. Generally, many books give a very rigid explanation of the bardo saying that it lasts forty-nine days and the bardo body is reborn every seven days. Actually, it is not necessarily like that. The bardo stage can sometimes be very short. It is not a fixed state of seven days. The seven days we are talking about are calculated based on our time. The concept of time and space in the bardo, in the heavens, in the hells, are all relative and not the same. For example, in our lives, the happiest times seem to fly by in minutes but actually a few hours have passed. When in pain, sickness, and suffering, one minute, even one second, seems to last a long time. So time is relative. When you are in your glory, the time feels very short; when you are in pain, the time feels very long.

Therefore, in the bardo stage, although it is said that there is a death and rebirth every seven days, the so-called seven days is not calculated in the fixed time of our world. In these seven days, what realm appears, whichever bodhisattva comes to welcome you...whatever god comes to pull you, whether Allah, Buddha, etc., in fact, is all relative. Fixed times are just a convenient way of explaining, it is not definitive. This will be discussed further later.

So why does the bardo body go through such a big change every seven days? We haven't talked about life yet! Life in the womb also goes through big changes every seven days. Being alive now in this human world, we go through a big change every seven days, but no one knows it. Therefore, to truly learn Chinese and Western medicine, one must understand this. For example, if a person catches a cold, it takes three, seven, or twenty-one days before the cold can be completely uprooted. Taking medicine is just to help ease your symptoms. The cold actually changes every seven days.

"The longest that the bardo existence lasts is forty-nine days," is also a bit of a contrived statement. Nowadays, there are people who make a living "communicating with the other side." There are mediums and channelers who call the souls of your ancestors to talk to you. And there are people who channel the gods and dance. Do you think those people are actually communicating with the bardo person? They're not. That is completely the Alaya Consciousness. The Alaya Consciousness of the medium or channeler dialogues with the Alaya Consciousness of the person you want to communicate with. It is completely an illusion, it is not actually real. Those who study Buddhism laugh heartily when they hear about these things, but most people believe it very much.

After Buddhism entered China, the practice of chanting for

the deceased every seven days for forty-nine days to help them gain liberation during the bardo existence. The principle of doing it for this long is just in case the person should remain in the bardo the entire length of time. Does the bardo existence really have such an exact fixed time? There is no such thing.

We will finish up here today. I haven't talked about rebirth yet. Do you have any questions? Feel free to discuss among yourselves, I will be listening.

Session Four

Master Nan: Mr. Xu, good that you are here. Please talk about your "death" experience. I'll take a short break. He is very interesting, this old friend from Shanghai. There's a very funny story. Because of his experience, he thinks death is a good thing. So when one of his relatives died and someone called to inform him, he said "That's great news!" His mother was furious and lambasted him.

Xu: This is my own personal experience. I specifically consulted Master Nan about it two years ago. Master found it funny.

Master Nan: Very special.

Xu: It was like this, when I was about forty years old, I went to a dinner party. I can usually drink one to two bottles of rice wine, but I only drank a little that day because I was really tired. My chest suddenly felt suffocated, I broke out in a cold sweat, and felt extremely uncomfortable. I just fell forward onto the table, it looked like I was resting.

At this time, my consciousness was very clear. I suddenly flew upward in a snap. I felt that this must be the soul. I was floating in an environment where two-thirds were mountains and one-third was sky. I'd never felt such clarity. It was very quiet, there was no sound at all, there was no noise at all, just floating there. The mountains were blurry, with a little bit of dark green and the sky also had just a little color, like a blurry ink painting. I'm just floating there, I can't see my shape, but I'm very clear, just floating and comfortable. It seems that every cell is completely relaxed. To a person who is alive, there is no way to describe this wonderful feeling, a kind of complete relief, and the thinking is clear and concentrated, as if lying on an extremely high silk cotton quilt, floating...floating...floating...

Normally, I love my daughter very much, but during this time, I didn't think of her. If I thought of her occasionally, it seemed like we merely knew each other but had no more emotional connection. It seemed as if there was a few generations of separation between us. This kind of floating...floating... Suddenly, I realized that I was going back, and I immediately regretted this! Then "pop" all of a sudden, I was back.

After I came back, I lifted my head up and looked. It was like nothing was going on, and I couldn't think of why I was sitting there today. Later, I recognized that I was eating. I said, I'm sorry, I just didn't feel well. They were not surprised, thinking I was tired, so they just let me rest for a while. Afterwards I asked the person next to me, how long did I pass out? He said about a minute or two.

I didn't believe in souls, or spirits, or ghosts, or gods before! I grew up with a materialist education. From this time on, I have felt that there must be a soul, and this level of comfort is indescribable in worldly terms. It is not like being hungry, wanting to eat a meal, and then having a piece of meat, or abalone. It's not that kind of feeling. Rather, it's a kind of eternal, complete liberation and contentment. This kind of contentment is not normal happiness or giddy joy, but a very quiet, comfortable, well-being. Because I had this experience, I am sure that it was not a fantasy. I am sure that it's not like the modern explanations, the so-called temporary illusions caused by nerves. They say, when people faint in pain, there is a counter reaction and there is a feeling of comfort, no. At that time, my thinking was very clear and complete.

At that time, I realized that Xu is just a name given to my soul. Because I was outside of the body, my thoughts are very complete, there is no lack at all, and I am so clear. I am just so floating...

I feel that I have confirmed many things, one is that there must be a soul and confirming that there are souls that explain a lot. As well, there are so-called gods, there are so-called ghosts, there are so-called...whatever you call them, they are kind of the same thing. No matter what you call it, it absolutely does exist.

I took a cursory look at the various religious doctrines and they all seemed similar. Christianity says that people have original sin, and how to do good in this world; Buddhism says turn back to arrive at the shore, and so on. I'm thinking, it seems that the main starting point and destination of religions is actually just teaching people to be compassionate, and then the soul is saved. No matter what it says, "saved" or whatever, and can finally ascend to heaven. Where is heaven? I don't know. Did you go to another space? Where do you finally go? I do not know either.

Later I looked at the "Near Death Studies." There are tens of thousands of cases in the United States. They are generally similar with minor differences. The main feeling is one of joy and liberation. Then everyone has their personal experience. Some entered the tunnel, some heard wonderful music, and some visited friends and relatives they wanted to see. I realized that they are all real, and the most important point is that they all had a sense of relief or liberation, a sense of eternity, which must be real, because I have already experienced it myself. After experiencing it, I discovered that both materialism and idealism are actually the same thing, in fact they are both materialism. Physicality that exists in another space is objective and not fictional. We are now in a three-dimensional space plus time. The so-called four-dimensional world, the so-called *yang*(as opposed to *yin*) world, must have many dimensions of space and must have souls or beings, but our *yang* world cannot detect these yet.

Later, I found out that Teacher Nan also summarized life, old age, sickness and death, life and death, and so many painful things. There are so few happy things, happy things are very short-lived, but painful things happen often and universally, and they are quite eternal. It's like, for example, I'm hungry and uncomfortable. I feel a little better after eating a piece of bread, right? Well, after eating too much, you feel uncomfortable. There are many painful things, if you fall down when you are walking, it hurts. I found that being alive is laborious, which will not bring you happiness.

So, one of my uncles died, and I said oh this is a good thing, very good. He was born with serious diabetes. Later in life, he got an infection and died within two or three days. I think this is a good thing. The torture that people suffer when they are about to die is beyond the total amount of pain experienced throughout their lifetime. Such an easy, swift death was the result of his cultivation. So I said, this is a good thing, very good. When I told Master Nan about it, Master Nan laughed.

Master Nan: Mr. Xu, if you are hot, take off your coat, put it on your shoulders, sit comfortably, cross-legged or not, it doesn't matter. Take a rest, listen in, or meditate, whatever you want.

We'll continue speaking, you are completely free.

Today, I will continue the talks that I did not finish yesterday. This time it's because of Hu Songnian's request. I was working just now because I received a pile of greeting cards during the Chinese New Year, and I don't know how to deal with them. It's a big headache to receive all these greeting cards and letters. Friends, please help me out, don't write letters or send greeting cards. It's not good for me to reply, nor is it good if I don't reply. I won't reply to many of them. I don't know how much time and energy will be wasted if I continue this.

New Year's cards probably only started in the Republic of China a few decades ago. There were no New Year cards in ancient China until the end of the Manchu Qing Dynasty. At that time, it was an agricultural society with inconvenient transportation, so intellectuals had to write a letter to pay new year's respects.

Later, printing developed and there were New Year cards, but now there are more and more. I think this waste is terrible. At first I also replied, but the more I thought about it, the less I would reply. I think this is wasteful of people. It seems to be polite but it's unreasonable. It's really troublesome for the Chinese to celebrate the New Year. It's Christmas, then western New Year, and then Chinese lunar New Year's greetings. It's more and more trouble, and there is no set of customs and politeness. This is just an aside.

The weather in the afternoon was not good, I really didn't want to talk. I didn't have enough energy, I am really getting old. But I had agreed, so I went on with it.

Both Xu and Wang both had death experiences. Let me add two words, "self proclaimed" experiences of death. How should I put this? They think it was death. I will explain later, I don't agree that they died, they didn't really die, those were just near death experiences. This is what I had mentioned yesterday, passing out is one of the states of no-mind in Buddhism, similar to death, but not death.

The consciousness has not completely separated from the body, nor completely separated from the brain. In other words, it is very difficult to say for sure and a scientific experiment should be done to explain it better. Science is also an assumption, at least so far, but this may not be true in the future. Don't believe it completely. What I'm talking about is also an assumption. Let's assume that consciousness can be counted as one hundred units. Xu reported his own experience just now. If 60%, or even up to 70%, of his consciousness left the body, the remainder of his consciousness is still in the body. In other words, only the part of his consciousness that is in the brain has shut down, doesn't know anything, is passed out. However, the part of the consciousness that left is awake. And because there are no physical obstacles, it is very awake, like a bird out of the cage, very free, very comfortable, and very peaceful. This is also because his merits are good, not everyone is like this.

It would be better to have an instrument to test similar situations in the future. The consciousness does not completely detach from the brain, part of it remains in the left brain and in the back of the brain, similar to a lucid dream. So, in terms of his state, that was the unmitigated state of unconsciousness or coma no-mind state, the second of the five states of no-mind mentioned earlier. It was not the dhyana of no-thought no-mind state, it was not the dhyana heaven of no-thought no-mind state, it was not *nirodha samāpatti* no-mind state and it was not death, not real death. You should pay attention to these five states of no-mind.

"five grounds of no-mind": 1) deep, dreamless sleep no-mind state 2) unmitigated state of unconsciousness or coma no-mind state 3) the dhyana of no-thought no-mind state 4) the dhyana heaven of no-thought no-mind state 5) *nirodha samāpatti* (the cessation of perception, feelings and consciousness samadhi) no-mind state.

What is a state of no-mind? It means that the consciousness does not move. One is the deep, dreamless sleep no-mind state, second is the unmitigated state of unconsciousness or coma no-mind state, third is the dhyana of no-thought no-mind state, fourth is the dhyana heaven of no-thought no-mind state and fifth is *nirodha samāpatti* (the cessation of perception, feelings and consciousness samadhi) no-mind state. During both death and birth, there are short periods of no-mind. The dhyana of no-thought is a state attainable through practice. It is not orthodox samadhi, but it is a very high attainment. Buddha Shakyamuni also learned the dhyana of no-thought. After achieving this, he gave it up recognizing that it was the wrong path. The dhyana of no-thought is a high-level of dhyana of the Form Realm. The function of thinking is shut down, but it is not Tao, not Nirvana.

For example, as he just described, when Mr. Xu passed out, was he in a state of no thinking? No, there was still thinking, it was certainly not a state of no-mind. But his thinking, his sixth consciousness seemed to be partially separated from the body.

If we informally look at how medicine talks about this, in ancient China, it was called "hun-soul escape syndrome"(離魂症). My 'if' is also a scientific assumption. There is an ancient book that tells a very good literary story called "The Girl Whose Hun-Soul Left", which is very famous in Chinese literature. In the book, two cousins are in love, but the family opposes their relationship.

Lu Fangweng and Tang Wan were also cousins who married. As a result, after getting married, Lu Fangweng's mother didn't like this daughter-in-law. She originally chose her niece to be daughter-in-law, and finally forced Lu Fangweng to divorce. The famous book, "Chai Tou Feng," is the poems written by Lu Fangweng, and Tang Wan's poems in response. In the end, their poem dialogue was passed down in the history of Chinese literature and is very famous.

Now I'm going to talk about the story of Qian Nu's hun-soul leaving her. It's a story from the Tang Dynasty. The parents opposed the marriage of the two cousins. Even so, the female cousin felt she absolutely must marry this older male cousin. One day, this girl ran away to be with her cousin, the two got married and lived together, true story. More than ten years had passed since she left. After such a long time, the girl still missed her parents and went back to her family home. Upon return, she scared the family to death. Why? Because this daughter had been asleep in her bed for more than ten years, not quite dead, not quite alive, just laying there. The daughter was stunned when she heard this. The family brought her into the room, isn't this you sleeping here? Puff, this girl disappeared and the one in the bed was awake. In the end, the two cousins became a couple.

In Chinese medicine, there is also sleepwalking syndrome, somnambulism, and many people are affected by this. When I was young, I saw with my own eyes, there was a guy, I forget what we called him, from the countryside. He carried water to my house. We all knew that he would also carry water at night. He has no knowledge of this. He would sleep until midnight, put on his clothes, and fetch water for everyone. He would open the door of your house and fill the water for you, and then he would go to sleep again. The next day, he didn't know that he had already filled the water. This is somnambulism.

When I led soldiers, I paid great attention to this matter. Leading troops in the army, what are you most afraid of? The commander is most afraid of a "troublesome camp," also known as an "agitated camp." For example, if the unit went to a remote place and had no place to camp, they would stay in an ancestral temple. I would personally check it first, to see which the most dangerous and terrifying areas were. I would light a fire, or take some dry grass and smoke those areas. My thinking was a bit old-school. I am burning this incense for you, lonely souls and wild ghosts, so please leave this place. The soldiers were not allowed to sleep in those places. I slept there on my own. I was still a little bit scared, but the seriousness of leading the soldiers kept that in check. Sometimes there were hundreds of people encamped, and someone would suddenly get up at night, take a gun, start loading it with bullets, and scream, "Charge! Charge!" All the other soldiers woke up and followed suit, getting their guns and bullets. At this time, it is very important for the commander to be calm and wise. First instruct the trumpeters, "Blow the horn! Troops gather!" The soldiers lined up with their guns, "Attention! About face! March to your beds! Go to sleep!" They all put down their guns and go back to sleep, it's over. If you don't have the experience to deal with this, people will fire their guns indiscriminately. If they think they see the enemy in front of them, it could be a disaster. Another army leader encountered an "agitated camp" and because the commander got shaken up by the experience, he was defeated in battle.

I don't know whether or not present day military education talks about these things. We didn't talk about those things in the old military school. Back then they were all secret but everyone knew. Anyone who was going to lead the army should know those things. They affect everyone. The sleepwalking soldier loaded his gun with bullets, as if he was awake but he was actually dreaming! This is what's called somnambulism.

I see that currently there are many medical cases which society calls mentally illness and medicine calls schizophrenia. Don't be afraid of schizophrenia, you have to know that it is a result of a dichotomy between the nerves in the brain and thoughts. This topic requires a study of the brain. I'm going off on a tangent again, but at this point, I will share with you more experience. When you go to see a doctor, "ear, nose, and throat" is one department and is concerned with a particular set of nerves. Eyes are not included in this, ophthalmology is ophthalmology, and its nerve routes are different. When you meditate and repair the qi mai, the nerves of the left brain, right brain, forebrain, and back brain are different, and the routes of thought and consciousness are also different. So don't think of the name schizophrenia as mental illness. A person who really knows how to cultivate and who understands medicine can see that the thoughts of many 'normal' people, even many big bosses, scholars, executives, and many great people, are in fact, 'schizophrenic'. While teaching classes at the Army University, we paid great attention to the students. For example, we had a student who was a major general. We secretly created a record about him because he had mental problems and could not lead troops. He could only serve as a staff member. Leading troops would cause problems because his mental pathways and thinking were different. This is a science which involves many things.

Speaking of this, Mr. Xu's report of his experience is real. His nose is blocked. He has very serious rhinitis which affects his brain. I did not carefully study whether it is the left or right nostril. The nerves are crossed, if the right nostril is blocked and the left brain is affected, and if the left nostril is blocked and the right brain is affected.

So I thought, after arriving at Miaogang, I will set up a

specialized laboratory and buy equipment to research the brain. The attainments of dhyana in meditation are absolutely related to the brain. The core of a person's health lies in the brain, and a person's brain is really not mature until s/he is sixty to sixty-five years old. This is just in terms of the brain! Materially speaking, it is similar to how an apple matures. I have said that human life is very pitiful, and the brain is not sound at birth, and it does not mature until old. Look at Eastern and Western cultures, science is so advanced, and religious philosophy is so advanced. The amount of our brain that we use throughout our lives is really only a small percentage, only a tiny portion. This is not about thinking or consciousness, thinking and consciousness function using the nerves of the brain, using circuits. That's why spiritual cultivation can give rise to supernatural powers you know.

It can also be said that Mr. Xu saw another time and space. That is to say, a certain part of the brain which was normally not functioning, opened a little at that time.. Therefore, from a materialistic point of view, true supernatural powers, or the wisdom of enlightenment are all related to the brain, very intricately related.

Therefore, physically, the focus of the so-called "returning the energy and replenishing the brain, brings longevity and immortality" of the Taoists, is on the brain. The brain is related to the mind and consciousness. The examples of Mr. Xu's account of his soul going out of the body, schizophrenia, somnambulism, and "hun-soul escape syndrome"(離魂症) I mentioned just now are all related to the brain. Here you need to pay special attention: thinking and consciousness are not produced by the brain, but for people who are alive, the thinking consciousness works by the brain's electrical circuits, so the condition of the brain has an impact on thinking consciousness.

Some intelligent people, we have a lot of them here, recognize that when they are thinking deeply about something, they sometimes forget about themselves until suddenly — yo!— they're back. A small part of the yang-spirit was out wandering. That part of the consciousness detached while thinking. In the Consciousness Only School, this phenomenon is called "single-headed consciousness." The consciousness is operating alone. Though it seems to have separated from the brain, there is no actual detachment. The single-headed consciousness is also called the "solitary shadow consciousness," a state of focus on internal images. Just now, what Mr. Xu described shows that he had entered this state.

When some people meditate, whether they study Buddhism or Taoism, they will enter a state of "soul out of body" which feels very comfortable. In Taoist practice, it is called the "yin-spirit leaves the body, 陰神出竅." Why is it called the yin-spirit? Let's take Mr. Xu's account as an example. In terms of scientific logic, we fully accept that Xu's account was really his experience and he didn't make it up. Scientifically we will assume it to be true. In his account, the 'Mr. Xu' who had gone out of the body was in the air. He turned and saw mountains that looked like a pale ink painting, hazy and unclear. In other words, he himself seemed to be above, in a special space, in another world, very comfortable, and no worries in his heart. He mentioned that he thought about his favorite daughter but it was merely a thought that arose in his consciousness. It was as if there were several lives of distance between them, as if the relationship was almost irrelevant, totally unlike their actual relationship in this life. So did the Mr. Xu of that state have an actual physical form? No, he didn't. That is why it was a yin-spirit.

What is a yang-spirit? If you practice dhyana meditation, after a certain level of attainment, you can deliberately create one or more of "you," and others can see them. According to the Taoist formula, you "build a foundation in a hundred days, get pregnant in October, breastfeed for three years, and face the wall for nine years." Taoists say, "refining the vital energy returns it to qi; refining the qi returns it to spirit; and refining the spirit returns it to voidness." This part of Taoism is no different from Buddhism, but Taoism talks about it from the material standpoint, from actual experience and achievement. Buddhism goes more into the principles. What is yang-spirit? It means to create another person. For example, the person is at home, working in an office, and talking to a child; at the same time, that person is sitting here with us. We can shake hands with and talk with this person. It is like a clone, physically tangible. There are people who have reached this point. If you ask him, he won't tell you. He'll just smile and say that there is no such thing, that you got it wrong. He won't admit it.

For example, I often mention people from Confucianism. After the Song Dynasty, Zen Buddhist and Taoist practice methods were integrated into their writings, and they also had very high achievements. But this part is ignored by current scholars. There are many books of this kind, and there are many experiences. They talk about how to be a man and do things and talk about cultivation. Look at the "Ming Confucian Case," about a Confucian in the Ming Dynasty, Mr. Luo Jinxi, a native of Nancheng, Jiangxi. He was very famous and was familiar with Confucianism, Taoism and Buddhism. He had a very high level of cultivation. He predicted the time and day he would die. More than a month after his death, a fellow villager saw him in the Jiangsu area and said, "Hey, Mr. Luo, you are here!" "Yes, yes, oh you are here!" The two had a conversation and asked after their respective families. When the villager went back and told people in the village, they said, "Don't talk nonsense, Mr. Luo has been dead for more than a month." This belongs to the category of yang-spirit.

The yin and yang are just symbolic names not having any special meaning. One is tangible and has form, so it is called yang-spirit. One has no form or appearance and is called yin-spirit. There are so many stories like these in Taoism.

There is a Taoist saying that criticizes the general Buddhist practitioner who meditates, or practices Chan/Zen or recites the Buddha's name, and as well the criticism includes ordinary Taoist practitioners. They say: "Cultivating this life but not true nature; This is the first illness of practice." Some practitioners are keen on practicing Qi and energy channels. They work hard to open the two main channels, Governing and Reproductive (Ren and Du). Their practice focuses on the body. This is just cultivation of this life, not true nature. It does not involve knowing the mind, does not lead to awakening or enlightenment. This is the first illness of cultivation. This kind of cultivation is going the wrong way, and it falls into grasping the view of the body as self.

"But if you cultivate your ancestral nature without cultivating alchemy, it is difficult for the spirit to enter the sacred even after a thousand eons." For example, many people who study Buddhism only talk about theories, have a mouth full of chan, but have no change in their bodies. They may have had a little bit of an awakening, but are not able to stay out of ignorance continuously, moment-by-moment. They are not concerned with the transformation of this body so their essence, energy and spirit can not be condensed into one. This is at best only half of cultivation. It can produce a yin-spirit, but not a yang-spirit. It is only during the bardo stage that a yang-spirit can be achieved. During their lifetime, they will not achieve the sambhogakaya or the nirmanakaya.

The sambhogakaya achievement is to transform this retribution body. The yang-spirit is a nirmanakaya achievement. Without relying on a mother, one can give birth to another life, and others can see this incarnation. We are usually born from a woman's womb, but if one succeeds in cultivating a yang-spirit, this new self is born from the top of our head. Taoism and Tantric cultivation are almost the same line. This should not be discussed as part of this class. Today because Mr. Xu talked about his near-death experience, I opened my chatterbox all the way and told you about it.

For example, some of you here often play around with these things, play around with yin-spirit, help others check into this and that. Playing around with the yin-spirit for a long time is very detrimental to you. You will end up going into the ghost realm and will become a spirit ghost in the future. For example, Wang Yangming was a great Confucian. He had studied Buddhism and Confucianism, and had supernatural powers. In Wang Yangming's case, he also played with magical powers, but in the end he discarded them. Wang Yangming was far more capable than all of you. A friend of his wanted to see him and travelled a long distance. Wang already knew. On that day, he went out a few miles distance to wait for his friend. His friend said, I came to see you, why are you here? He said, I came to meet you. His friend thought it was strange: How did you know that I would be here? He said, I knew a long time ago. However, Wang Yangming gave this up later. He said, "This is just playing with the spirit!" So, take a look at Wang Yangming's case, he followed the Confucian way.

Wang Yangming was a very interesting person for his day. The Japanese Meiji Restoration was influenced by his philosophy, thinking, and writings, which was called Wang Studies. Chiang Kai-shek also studied Wang Studies. Wang Yangming used to be the governor of Jiangxi. At that time, a governor controlled the political party, government and army, and thus had more power than today's governors. There is a story in another biography of Wang Yangming about an incident which occured when he went to a temple in Jiangxi. He felt that the temple was very impressive, however, there was a locked room there. He asked a monk why this room was locked. The monk said that long ago there was an old monk who was in retreat and died, attaining nirvana, in there. He ordered the door to be locked and to not be opened. When Wang Yangming heard this, he figured there was a problem! He said there is something strange going on in this temple, maybe some secret agent is inside, or a monk is doing bad things and deceiving people. He was the highest authority of the area and ordered the door to be opened! He wanted to take a look. The monk said we must never open this room. Two or three generations of patriarchs have ordered that this room cannot be opened. The more he heard, the stranger it seemed. Wang Yangming's personality being what it was, this got his goat! He had to open it, "Open it for me immediately!" Asserting his authority, the monk had no choice but to open it. When opened, he found a skeleton sitting in meditation position. There was a note on the table in front of him. It said "Wang Shouren, the one who opened the door is the one who closed the door fifty years ago." Wang Yangming's name is Wang Shouren, Yangming is his courtesy name. He was dumbstruck. Oh, it turns out he is me! In his previous life, he had achieved his Nirvana here. His accomplishment was very advanced. He foresaw that upon reincarnation, he himself would open this door. But within Confucianism, this koan was not accepted and recorded. Confucianism took away many true stories, thinking they were too mysterious. They were afraid of criticism.

Mr. Xu, who reported his near death experience to you, has a friend whose surname is Wang, who also "died". Can you (Xu) tell everyone his story?

Xu: At that time, Wang had stomach problems. He had a bleeding ulcer and his blood pressure dropped to forty. He fainted suddenly, and similar to me, it felt like his soul left the body. He said he saw a garden, the sun was shining, there were pavilions, and music. He floated just above the treetops... He finally floated to the front, and there was a hazy little house. Inside it was dark, he stayed there and refused to go in. But there was a voice, a force pushing him in, absolutely forcing him to go in. I asked him, "what sound did you hear?" He said that he couldn't remember. Maybe it wasn't a sound. It was someone who meant, "Go in, go in." As soon as he entered, he woke up. His time [in that state] lasted longer [than mine].

Master Nan: Wang is an electrical engineer. At his age, they were all educated as a generation of materialists, and originally didn't believe this stuff.

Session Five

Master Nan: We talked about the normal course of a person's death yesterday. But there is one thing, everyone must pay attention. I often find that when most people are listening, their minds are not logical enough, and they can't grasp the main point. They get carried away by the extraneous material. Therefore, to learn, you must be scientifically minded and understand logic first. Yesterday we talked about normal human death and the dissipation of the four elements. Keep this in mind. If you understand logic, you can see that this is a small topic within the larger topic of life and death, and it is limited to the normal death of human beings. At the same time, use your wisdom to ponder whether abnormal deaths, as well as the deaths of other sentient beings are the same or not? Because time is limited, these questions are outside the scope of our discussion. Don't think that the life and death of every sentient being is so normal, and it is all too difficult to die a normal death.

We learn after teaching for a long time that if a hundred students listen to a class, what they write down is not what the teacher said. Everyone catches a little bit and runs with it. So I have come to the conclusion, education is useless theory.

The same is true for teaching in ordinary schools. Starting from elementary school, why do some students in a class have good grades and some bad? Because some students' thinking is not logical enough, they are not with the program, and can't grasp the main idea. They are playing with their own subjective ideas while listening. This is a very serious matter, but now I bring it to everyone's attention.

Yesterday we only discussed the dissipation of the four elements and the arisal of the bardo body. I used words and words to tell you, which is the so-called reasoning of spoken language. In class yesterday, I taught you four reasonings: the reasoning of spoken language, the reasoning of observation, the reasoning of verification and attainment, and the reasoning of Thusness. The reasoning of spoken language is expressed in words; for example, I asked Xu to give his account earlier. This is the reasoning of observation. Within science, this would be part of the statistics of data and cases. Therefore, the study of things is observational and is relative, not absolute, not certain.

"Bardo" is a Buddhist term, and there is another term "suspension" (lit. 'middle stop' zhongzhi 中止). This was in the first translation of part of the Yogacarabhumi Sastra into Chinese. The term was not translated into "bardo" or "middle existence." In order to talk about practice, the first translation used "suspension," meaning that life is like flowing water divided into segments, flowing from the past to the present, and now stopping him in the middle. Yesterday is yesterday, tomorrow is tomorrow, today's existence is "suspended here," so it was called "suspension".

In the past, the translation of suspension was in popular use but it was overthrown by later generations. Later, the twelve interdependent links formalized the translation of 'existence' as the character "有," signifying 'now existing in the real world'. Another reason is because the concept of a human is a "human being." In terms of ontological principles and concepts of Buddhism, the real world is also illusory and unreal. Therefore, since it was settled that the term "being" would be used in the twelve interdependent links, the use of "suspension" was stopped and changed to "middle existence/being".

So why is it called bardo (lit. middle yin)? Just now I said that in Chinese, this is also justified. Everything is relative. On one side, there is the obviously visible and tangible, called yang; on the other is the invisible and intangible called yin. Therefore, the middle existence is also called the "middle yin" or bardo, which we commonly call "*ling-hun*, 靈魂," the spirit-hun or soul. For example, in Xu's account earlier, the 'soul' went out, he felt 'something' go out. Because he is Chinese, his thinking is affected by education and concepts and he calls this 'something', *ling-hun*, which is also a hypothetical name. This is what it is commonly called in Chinese, but not in Buddhist culture. The so-called *ling-hun* is very sensitive, knows almost everything, knows everything, has feelings, and has perception, but he is not a physical thing.

In regards to the source of Chinese characters for *ling-hun*, 靈魂, the character for *hun,* 魂, is made up of the character for "ghost"鬼 next to the character for "cloud"云. Ghosts are within the yin realm and are invisible whereas gods are in the yang realm and are visible. If we study these two characters carefully, both ghost 鬼 and god 神 are both related to land, to cultivated fields 田 specifically. Within the character for ghost, the field has lines that extend down into the ground representing the yin aspect of electrical current going down into the ground. On the top, there is one hair-like stroke representing the hairs on your head standing up. This is the composition of the character for the word ghost 鬼. In the character for the word god 神, in the middle of the right side is the field. On the left side is *"shi,"*示 meaning reveal or manifest, which belongs to the heavens. Above and below the field are lines of extension that become *"shen"*申. This is the composition of the character for the word "god." When you add a line going upward from the character *"tian"*田, which represents the land, it is called *"you"*由 which means budding—things are starting to grow up toward the light in the field. If there are lines going both upward and downward from the field, this is the base of the character for the word *"shen"*申, stretch or reach—reaching all directions, everywhere above and below. Add the character for reveal/manifest next to this, what the heavens manifest or reveal is called god 神.

On the right side of the character for *hun,* 魂 , is the

character for ghost [which contains the character for cloud on the lower right hand side]. If ghosts are connected downward but not upward, why add a cloud? This is the abbreviated character of cloud. One could say, they are just like clouds and mist, which seem to exist and seem to be nothing. They are blurry and vague so they are called *hun*.

There is a difference between *hun* 魂 and *po* 魄. The *"po"* is material and physical. We have physical energy, *qi*. Just like in the north when we breathe in cold air, we breathe out white breath. *Po* are substantive, are material; *hun* do not have substance. They are invisible, and nebulous like clouds. *Hun-po* 魂魄 are two different things. When a person gets a fright, in literature this is described as "the *hun* has flown and the *po* have scattered." The *hun* flies out, the spirit of consciousness has left the body. As well, the body, the *po*, are frightened; the person pees their pants and trembles. It is the function of the physical body. The four great elements are in discord, and have somewhat separated. This is what is called "the *hun* has flown and the *po* have scattered."

So, if you look at ancient Chinese characters, every character has its scientific reasoning. Advocating simplified characters has created a big mess.

Let's not get carried away. Let's get back to the bardo. Life sciences are now studying this and a lot of information has been found, based on the reasoning of karma over lifetimes.

The bardo person can remember many things about their life. There is a saying in Chinese which is very simple, "a soul is not ignorant." The soul has this ability to remember. There is no ignorance, and no obscurity. They still remember. This is what is meant by "a soul is not ignorant." After the death of the average person, *"the hun flies away and the po disperse."* If there is a bardo stage, even if there is the state of no ignorance, it is only for the equivalent of less than a day in our world. After a few hours, the bardo person is ignorant again, which is equivalent to sleeping, passing out, and forgetting.

So why do you need to practice samadhi? From literature, if you have cultivated to the point that you have no ignorance, Confucians describe this as "very bright, very clear" (*zhaozhao lingling* 昭昭靈靈). *Zhaozhao* is very bright, and *lingling* is very clear. The faculties of seeing, hearing, feeling and perceiving are not obscured and there is no ignorance.

What is samadhi? It is the state of being neither distracted and confused, nor groggy. In other words, it is what Confucianists and Neo-Confucianists call *zhaozhao lingling*. It is not ambiguous, clear and clear, without delusions or distracting thoughts. The Buddha is awake. Awake means to be awakened from sleep, enlightened, in a state of clarity. To 'awaken from sleep' is enlightenment, and 'sleep' is a state of darkness and bewitchment [literally]. The Buddha is one who is always awake, who is not ignorant, who is "very bright, very clear," and not distracted, confused or groggy. Ordinary people can't do this. So meditating and cultivating samadhi is what you need to do. This is a supplementary explanation.

After the bardo body arises and wakes up, there is some lucidity. Therefore, other practice books describe that a spiritual light shines and passes in a flash. In fact, the bardo rises up like a dream. That was where we stopped yesterday, right? At this stage, when waking up after a coma, there is a saying in China, "You don't recognize your soul when you are alive, and you don't recognize your corpse when you die." We are alive and we don't recognize our own soul, unless you meditate and work hard to achieve the state of no ignorance. It is only after "seeing" clearly that one understands what happens when one's mind goes into the state of "soul" or ling-hun. After most people die, their bardo does not recognize their own body.

In Buddhism, the functions of the soul/*ling-hun* fall within the scope of the skandhas of thought and volition. The skandha of thought is thinking and the skandha of volition is the range of life force. The emergence of bardo is the function of the skandha of volition, which is actually karma, and operates at   an incredible speed. At this time, just like watching a movie, you remember all the things you did in your life, the good and the bad, the virtuous and the evil, very fast, much faster than TV. The things in your life that you have suppressed into the subconscious, or have concealed, all come out. The retributions for good and evil are coming. All the times you have wronged others, have been honorable toward others, have compromised others, and been compromised by others all appear. Not only that, but even the actions of previous lives appear. At this time, the power of the volition skandha to activate thoughts and memories is called the functioning of karma, is called karma, and this power repeatedly comes forth. How to prove it? It is equal to our older people who have forgotten the current events, but the past events clearly appear. This is still alive! When it comes to the bardo, it is more serious than this. Not only did things from my childhood appear, but also from the previous life and many lives before that.

Now we ask a question, at this time, is there heaven and hell? Yes, the realm of heaven and hell can also appear. Are there any ghosts? Yes, they all appear, faster than in dreams, and many times faster than movies, television and computers.

But the Buddha tells you that there is no heaven, no hell, none of these things, that they are all functions of your mind, that all phenomena are manifestations of your mind. It is not only in the bardo state, but everything inside and outside of our body and mind while still alive, spiritual and material, is manifested by our mind. This "mind only" is the unity of mind and matter, which is the ontology spoken of in philosophy. No phenomena exist independent of original nature. Everything is the function and change phenomenon of the true nature. Whether we think this is true or not is all relative. Assumptions of our consciousness fall into the principle of observation and the principle of action, but not the principle of Thusness.

From the perspective of observation, various phenomena appear in the bardo realm because the person has these seeds in their consciousness, and these seeds burst forth. In this life as a human, why do we become a man or a woman? Each person has a different body, experience, and environment? These are the karmic results of multiple previous lifetimes, the seeds become activated. In the past, over many lives and eons, all our behavior and every action, virtuous, evil or neutral actions create a karmic force and form seeds (*bijas*). When the conditions are fully mature, the seed will become active. What one's lifetime entails, one's fate and luck, experiences, thinking patterns and emotional habits are all seeds which become the current behaviors and phenomena. What we have done throughout this life plus the accumulated habits of the sixth consciousness become the seeds of future lives stored in the Alaya Consciousness. So the currently active seeds give rise to seeds of the future—cause and effect happens like this. Many factors arise from cause and effect; cause and effect is too complicated, and even the most sophisticated computer cannot figure it clearly.

Therefore, from the perspective of the phenomenal and the observational, did the Buddha also say there is heaven and hell in the bardo at this time? Yes, both will appear.

If the person believes in Christianity, they will see the phenomena depicted by Christianity because these impressions exist in the consciousness. People of other religious beliefs see phenomena of other religious faiths. If the person is an atheist, they will see the images that normally occupy their consciousness. So it's not like, when the bardo rises, a certain bodhisattva will appear during the first seven days, and something else will happen during the second seven days... This is for people who study Buddhism or a certain sect because they grew up only seeing this, their environment is such, and they are accustomed to this. If the person didn't study this religion, and those paintings or statues weren't in the environment, what they see will not be this. Like Americans, they will see white angels appear, Mother Mary appear, or whatever ideal realm they have been imagining.

There is a problem in this, the Buddha said "not god, not nature." There is no Hades, God, Bodhisattva, or Buddha as your ruler. Your life all depends on the maturing of your own karma. The main point here is past, present and future causal relationships. Therefore, the Buddha has one of the most important instructions. The basis of the three-time-period connections of cause and effect is your psychological behavior and your day to day social behavior and deeds. The driving force behind this is the accumulated actions and behavior of countless lives from the past to the present. In modern terms, it is neither materialistic nor idealistic, but it also includes both materialistic and idealistic forces. This is called karma. As mentioned earlier, "karmic creation" includes three types of karma: virtuous, evil, and neutral. Neutral karma is ambiguous and sometimes we have no memory of it. Don't think that if you have no memory of something, it does not actually exist. It does exist and there will be retribution.

So why do we need to cultivate precepts, concentration and wisdom when studying Buddhism? This is a basic principle, and there is a verse everyone should pay attention to:

"Even though hundreds of eons have passed, karmic deeds are not forgotten; When the right conditions gather, the karmic results will still return to yourself."

Even after "hundreds of eons," no matter how long ago, how many tens of millions or billions of years, "karmic deeds are not forgotten." Your actions did not become forgotten or disappeared. "When the right conditions gather, the karmic

146

results will still return to yourself." The actions we do, whether in the physical world or in the spiritual world, everything that has been done, all things, are recorded. For example, when we were young, the most painful thing we encountered, our favorite things, things we will never forget, even if we don't usually think about them, still exist subconsciously. This is to say that if after a hundred eons, karma does not perish. There are no forgotten mistakes, they will always exist and so this is called "all existence," not "all emptiness." When the right conditions gather, you will receive this karmic result. This is how life and death come about.

There is also a verse in Buddhism:

"If you wish to know what happened in your past life, what you receive in this life shows it clearly. If you wish to know about your future life, the person of this life is its creator."

"If you wish to know what happened in your past life, what you receive in this life shows it clearly." He said that by observing your personality and experiences in this life, you will know what you have done in your previous life or however many previous lives before, so that you have these results in this life, and you can see the causes of the past by their fruits. "If you wish to know about your future life," people want to know about the next life or the next few lives? It is also very easy, "the person of this life is its creator." It depends on what you have done in this life. If you deceive someone, you will be deceived in the next life; if you kill someone, you must pay the debt of your own life in a future life. Everything, including love, everything has cause and effect.

The above two verses illustrate the three-time-periods of cause and effect, and the cycle of rebirth in the six realms.

Therefore, when the state of the bardo rises, you will find that not only the present lifetime, but all the things of past lives as well, scenes upon scenes flash by. How fast does it all happen? There is something commonly known to scientists that you should know. I would like to ask everyone present, how long does a person's dream last? The longest dream is less than five minutes. This is calculated based on the timescale of when we are awake, not the time in the dream.

For example, there are two famous dreams recorded in history, the dreams of Huang-liang and Nanke. There are two Huang-liang dreams, one is Lu Chunyang's Huang-liang Dream, by means of which Lu Chunyang was enlightened by Han Zhongli in Chang'an. Another Huangliang dream happened in Handan, Hebei, in the story of how Lu Chunyang, after his Taoist attainment, enlightened Lu Sheng.

Let's now talk about Lu Chunyang. Why did Lu Chunyang

become a monk? On his way to take the national exam, in Chang'an, Shaanxi, he was hungry and went into a restaurant. There was an old Taoist priest sitting there by himself cooking Huang-liang, millet rice. Lu Chunyang was so tired that he fell asleep as soon as he leaned on the table. He dreamed of the things that would happen in his life over the next decades. How he passed the exams and became an official, how he married his wife, had children, how he took pride in being an official, and rose in rank until he became the prime minister. In the end, his home was destroyed for having committed a crime and his family was exiled. In his old age, he was alone in the wind and snow, sighing and lamenting the futility of it all. He woke up, decades having clearly passed in front of his eyes. Looking up, the old Taoist priest on the other side smiled at him and asked, "Did you enjoy all that?" The old Taoist knew what he had dreamed about. Lu Chunyang saw that the old Taoist's millet rice was not yet cooked. Waking up, the millet was still not done, and within a few minutes, he had dreamed of decades of experiences. This is Lu Chunyang's Millet, Huang-liang, Dream.

Science now knows that the longest dream is less than five minutes. Sad and painful dreams, even the feeling of being pressed down in a dream, feel like they go on for a long time. Of course, there are often many dreams in one night, and most of us forget them when we wake up. Every dream is short, but in dreams, you feel as if a long time has passed, sometimes more than a few decades! So, time is relative.

There is also the Nanke Dream from the Tang Dynasty. There was a lazy man who wanted to be rich. One day after eating, he lay down in the yard and took a nap under a locust tree. He dreamed that he had arrived in the country of Huai'an (lit. Locust Peace) and met the princess. He boasted of how capable he was. In the end, he deceived the princess and became the magistrate. Not long after, an enemy country attacked and under his leadership, they were very quickly defeated. The princess committed suicide and the king expelled him from the country. After waking up, where is this country of Huai'an? Just two ant nests at war with each other under the locust tree. This is called "Nanke Dream", similar to the Huang-liang Dream. There is also the butterfly dream of Zhuangzi. These are famous dreams which tell us that life is like a dream, and dreams are like life.

Here let's take a detour to tell a little story. In literature, everyone bemoans that life is just a millet dream! In the Qing Dynasty, there was a scholar who failed the national exam. Arriving in Handan, he remembered the Millet Dream of Lu Chunyang, and full of sentiments, he wrote a poem:

Twenty years from entitlement to finish,
Although a dream, oh how epic!
I am down on my luck in Handan,

Mr. Lu may I borrow your pillow?

"Twenty years from entitlement to finish," in the Millet Dream, to just be granted such a high position, equal to the status of the founding fathers, is something incredible. "Although a dream, oh how epic!" You say that life is like a dream, but alas, I still want to have this dream! "I am down on my luck in Handan." I am a southerner. Today I am in Handan without any food, very pitiful, having failed the national exam. "Mr. Lu may I borrow your pillow?" Hey! Lu Chunyang, please lend me your pillow. I also want to have such a dream, my life will be fulfilled.

Looking at this poem, he is very erudite, and the artistic expression is very high. It represents life. It is said that because of public appreciation for this poem, this person really became an official and his career ended in tragedy. He got his wish and personally experienced a millet dream.

We now know that life is a dream, and we all want to live a good dream. So when I talk about philosophy in class, I often quote this "Mr. Lu may I borrow your pillow?" There are two famous lines in Chinese literature, which are also from the Qing Dynasty, "Since ancient times, passion leads to eternal regret and good dreams are the easiest to wake from." Like the Huangliang and Nanke dreams, they woke the dreamer up at once.

Returning to the bardo state, you should be aware that it's not like what is written in some books. In the first seven days, this bodhisattva will appear and you will experience this state; in the second seven days, that bodhisattva will appear to you...it's not so rigid and fixed. Are they right? Yes, within the scope of a certain religion and certain customs. Such people have not been exposed to the knowledge and world outside, and have always been in those halls from childhood to old age, and they have only seen those images. If you use this to save all sentient beings and use this theory to talk to others, it is not right.

For example, the Eskimos in the Arctic also have religious beliefs; in addition, the Manchus and Mongolians also have an ancient religion called Shamanism. For example, Japan is considered to be a Buddhist country. In fact, the state religion in Japan is "Shintoism." Buddhism is just one of the Japanese religions. Japanese people believe in Amaterasu. The true belief system of the majority of people is this polytheistic religion.

There are hundreds of religions in the world, and when people arise in the bardo state, they look similar to the way they did in life. The Chinese in recent decades have been educated in Marxist-Leninist ideological materialism. Those who have no contact with religious philosophy, their bardo state, dream state, only see things Marxist-Leninist style. I saw when old Communists were dying, they said, "Oh, I'm dying, I'm going to see Marx." That's right, because they have no other concepts, they deny religion. However, is it possible that a Buddha and Bodhisattva could appear to a materialist, or someone else, in the bardo after death? They might, because we can't guarantee that they didn't believe in Buddhism or another religion in their previous life. As I said earlier, the scenes which appear in the bardo are not just from this life, but from multiple lives, faster than dreams.

Everyone asks if there is really something behind fortune-telling or face reading? I said yes, because it was fixed karma from the past, showing up as karmic results of this life. For example, some people have nobility, wealth, and high position throughout their lives, but they constantly have bad luck and their health is not good. In addition, I know there were a few great people, including one who followed Sun Yat-sen in his revolution, a famous historical celebrity, who was born a eunuch, who was naturally impotent. Later, he adopted a daughter. There are many people who are born eunuchs. When I was in Sichuan, there was a rich man friend in Ziliujing. It was the richest place in Sichuan. Salt was produced there. This friend enjoyed wealth all his life, but he was also a "Natural Eunuch." He had this fame and wealth, but his body was like this.

Looking at many ancient heroes and talented people, they had very good luck, fame and wealth, but all of them had illnesses.

That is the ancient poem: "The thirty-six thousand days of a hundred years," there are only thirty-six thousand days within a life of a hundred years. "If not in distemper, then in illness doth pass." There are indeed people like this, and I have personally met some of these friends. What can be said? In terms of Buddhism,one's destiny in life is the result of the karma of many lives. That is to say, "Even though hundreds of eons have passed, karmic deeds are not forgotten; When the right conditions gather, the karmic results will still return to yourself."

I mentioned earlier, it is not a given that a particular bodhisattva or something will appear in the first seven days of bardo, and similarly during the second seven days; it's not necessarily like this. For example, a Tibetan who has been a monk since he was a child, or has practiced Buddhism in the same temple all his life would manifest that kind of realm—but I even hesitate to assert that. It is not necessarily gods or bodhisattvas who will appear in his bardo realm. There might be family members, because he also has family bonds, or he might have a love bond, and so on. So what will appear is varied and not fixed.

So for Catholics and people of other religions, will things always appear in line with that religion? Not necessarily, not every life. A person who is a Buddhist in this life might have believed in some cult or some other religion in their previous life.

What appears in the bardo state may even be related to something that happened in the previous life.

Karma is so difficult to explain clearly, it's too complicated, even a computer cannot calculate it. In regards to the so-called Six Paths of Rebirth, I usually tell practitioners to read the Surangama Sutra. The sections on rebirth in the six realms is explained simply and clearly, and scientifically. You monks talk about practice and cultivation, another very important sutra is the "Yogacarabhumi-sastra" which also talks about karmic results in relation to rebirth in the six realms. But I don't really like to extrapolate on these two because after you read them, you tend to observe others and make proclamations about this person's previous lives, or what will happen to this person in the next life. Everyone misinterprets, and forgets to reflect on themself, and only look at the faults of others. Like one of you here, who likes to close your eyes and talk nonsense. There is heavy karma for this. He doesn't realize that he has created negative karma of speech through saying all that nonsense.

Some of your (Hu Songnian) questions have already been answered along the way; other questions may or may not be answered. Maybe in the future, you know I am very busy here.

What about taking rebirth after death? Now, let's go back to that, I was starting to talk about this issue. At the very beginning,

I said that this time we will talk about life and death, but I am going to put the cart before the horse. Remember? We first talked about how people die, right? Now, that has all been explained clearly. What we are going to talk about next is how rebirth happens, and we will also only talk about normal rebirth of ordinary people.

Regarding this, Buddhism has a lot of material. The most important material for us to formally study this within Buddhism is the *Yogacarabhumi-sastra*. In fact, information in the translations from the Wei, Jin, Southern and Northern Dynasties to the Tang Dynasty, such as the "Da Ji Jing," is very scattered, one section here and another section there. They need to be studied together. Secondly, the Shurangama Sutra only talks about the larger principles of birth and death.

Before I talk about the issue of birth, I hope everyone will memorize the twelve links of interdependent arising (Pratītyasamutpāda), especially the lay practitioners, and for the ordained, this is even more important. This is intricately related to all Dharma practices, but most people don't remember it.

"Ignorance is a condition for volition. Volition is a condition for consciousness. Consciousness is a condition for name and form. Name and form are conditions for the six sense fields. The six sense fields are conditions for contact. Contact is a condition for feeling. Feeling is a condition for craving. Craving is a condition for grasping. Grasping is a condition for continued existence. Continued existence is a condition for rebirth. Rebirth is a condition for old age and death, sorrow, lamentation, pain, sadness, and distress to come to be."[4]

After you grow old, you die and after death you return again. This is the circle, the cycle of reincarnation, starting again from ignorance. You can also use one, two, three, four... to refer to the twelve links.

The so-called practice of life and death, meditation and concentration, especially those who become monastics, what do they do? Don't be mistaken. You think that meditation is to train your body and your spirit. Normally, if you say this, I have to smile, and I won't scold you. Strictly speaking, this is nonsense and you do not understand Buddhism. Buddhism is about understanding and becoming liberated from life and death. The so-called "understand life, escape death" are the four words to achieve; truly understand this life, and become liberated from sickness, suffering, old age and death. We must first clarify the

---

[4] "*Avijjapaccaya sankhara, sankharapaccaya vinnanam, vinnanam napaccay namarupam, namarupapaccaya salayatanam, salayatanapaccaya phasso, phassapaccayo vedana, vedanapaccayo tanha, tanhapaccayo upadanam, upadanapaccayo bhava, bhavapaccayo jati, jatipaccayo jaramaranam soka-parideva-dukkha-domanass-upayasa sambavanti. Evametassa kevalassa dukkha-khandhassa samudayo hoti.*" *(SN 12, 1)*

twelve links of interdependent arising. This is not a theory, but a science. It cannot be explained clearly even if we spent more than ten hours explaining it in detail. Much of it involves modern science, but nowadays Buddhist monks and lay people do not understand modern science, do not understand modern knowledge, just like me, so terrible! This is serious. This is why I said there is no way for Buddhism, for Buddhist studies, because most people don't know modern natural sciences and don't pay attention to them. They just hold on to Buddhism and think that they are the best, but they are trapped in a small range of knowledge, thinking they know everything.

The teachings of Mahayana and Hinayana practices, including Prajna teachings, Consciousness-only, Dhammalaksana, and Huayan, all developed based on the twelve links of interdependent arising. Everyone needs to be clear on this. The Buddha taught this to the Hinayana disciples who became monks with him. These disciples completely listened to his guidance. They did not apply other knowledge or ideals, but only focused on studying what the Buddha taught, and are called "Sound Hearers." The Sound Hearers were there to be educated, they had no independent thinking, and they didn't delve deep into investigation. What the Buddha said, they did. They just accepted whatever the teacher taught, and didn't have the ability to question. This is not the case with the Great Bodhisattvas. They may put forward their opinions and debate and challenge the Buddha.

The first of the twelve links of interdependent arising is "ignorance." This is the theory established by the Buddha. *Wuming* 無明, *avijja* in Pali, or in English, ignorance, literally means no light. The Chinese term *wu ming*, 無明, meaning 'no light,' falls in the category of *yin* (verses *yang*), meaning confused, knowing nothing. This term is often used in Buddhism. Yesterday I asked you about how you fall asleep and how you wake up. You don't know, and you are confused about it. That's 'moment-by-moment ignorance'. We are sitting here, and suddenly the thought of something far away pops up. You don't know where this idea suddenly came from, you were simply "thinking." Those who love to do business, you are meditating here, and suddenly think about flying to the United States where there is some business opportunity you almost forgot about. This is called 'moment-by-moment ignorance'. What's the mechanism behind why you suddenly think of something from ten years ago, or even from a past life? Sometimes our thoughts are connected to a past life. Something that we have never thought about or experienced, suddenly comes into the imagination. We chalk it up to imagination, in fact, it is connected to a previous life. This all falls within the range of 'moment-by-moment ignorance' arising.

This ignorance, from the perspective of Mind Only, is the

moment-by-moment ignorance of the mind and consciousness. What if you were out of the dark? Antara-Samyak-Sambodhi, great enlightenment, is finding the root of your existence. It is the opposite of this ignorance, this darkness; it is clarity, great light, great wisdom, the great mirror wisdom. But sentient beings don't understand, moment after moment, they remain in ignorance.

Here comes a scientific question in regards to the ignorance we mentioned just now. I am just sitting here comfortably, and something I never thought about suddenly pops up in my mind. Where did this come from? It comes from "volition", this moving force, driving force. "Volition" is karma. This force of karma is tremendous, always flowing, and is not obstructed by time and space. The Buddha explained the main points of life in one of the deepest and most secret sutras called the Saṃdhinirmocana Sūtra,[5] in which there is a verse, which tells the fundamental life of this one-minded ideal:

"The appropriating consciousness is profound and subtle indeed; all its seeds are like a rushing torrent. Fearing that they would imagine and cling to it as to a self, I have not revealed it to

---

[5] *Ārya-saṃdhi-nirmocana-sūtra* (traditional Chinese: 解深密經; ; pinyin: *Jiě Shēnmì Jīng*; Tibetan: དགོངས་པ་ངེས་འགྲེལ་ །, Wylie: *dgongs pa nges 'grel Gongpa Ngédrel*)

the foolish."[6]

"The appropriating consciousness [ādānavijñāna] is profound and subtle indeed." In the end, the Buddha overthrew all religions and all philosophies. There is no God, no Hades, no Shen, no personified god called Buddha, no master at all. The origin of life can be called by the name of "ādānavijñāna" and is also called "Ālaya-Vijñāna." Buddha said this thing, I can't explain it to you clearly, you won't understand. This appropriating consciousness [ādānavijñāna] is profound and subtle. It is very mysterious and difficult to understand.

"All its seeds are like a rushing torrent." What we call the past, the present and the future, is actually not limited by space and time. It is a unity of mind and matter. For example, the flow of the Hukou waterfall of the Yellow River and the flow of water at the Three Gorges in the Yangtze River, that power, that flow are the same. In the Mind-Only School of Buddhism, this flow is called "equal-flow," equally flowing. Look at the water in the Yellow River's waterfall, all those water molecules, in between them are sandwiched all that sand, and wood, and stuff. All the good, the bad, the virtuous, the evil, the neither-good-nor-evil, all the seeds of matter and the seeds of mind, there is no difference, they are all flowing together. Life in this universe has a power

---

[6] Keenan, John (2000), *Scripture on the Explication of the Underlying Meaning*, Berkeley: Numata Center, ISBN 1886439109 p.29.

that makes all seeds flow together equally. Mind and matter come from the same source. This power is "skandha of volition" and is the fundamental source of movement.

So does ancient Chinese culture have this idea? Yes it does! The "Book of Changes" tells you that "Heaven moves robustly" (*tian xing jian* 天行健) represented by the first hexagram ䷀ *qian gua*. This sky or heaven, 天, is not the scientific concept of sky, but an idea of heaven. It represents the noumenon, that is, the universe has power and is always in motion; material and spiritual functions have a dynamic force that is always changing.

This "skandha of volition" (行 *xing*) is the most difficult of the skandhas to understand. Spiritual practice is the cultivation of this! People talk about spiritual practice, but if you don't understand this, what kind of practice can there be! So the Book of Changes tells you "Heaven moves robustly." Then there was a sentence, "A gentleman continually strives for self-improvement." This sentence was added by Zhou Gong. While King Wen was studying the "Book of Changes," he had an enlightenment and wrote those three words about the *qian gua* 乾卦 (䷀) hexagram, "Heaven moves robustly." His son Zhou Gong studied the Book of Changes and added a sentence, "A gentleman continually strives for self-improvement." As human beings, we must understand the principles of the *qian gua* and understand that everything in the universe is changing at all times. Therefore, we must know how to self-improve, to be self-reflective at all times, to strive to cultivate knowledge, to continually improve, and not get deterred. That's why in the Great Learning it says "If each day is new, then every day is new, again a new day." That's where it came from. In later generations, quotes like "Learning is like sailing against the current, if you don't advance, you go backward," also come from this. The Diamond Sutra says, "Without dwelling, therein arises the mind" This is also based on the reality of the universe. All phenomena are changing at all times. What are you trying to hold onto!

"Fearing that they would imagine and cling to it as to a self, I have not revealed it to the foolish." The Buddha explained in the Saṃdhinirmocana Sutra and Surangama Sutra, which were some of the last ones, and the Saṃdhinirmocana Sutra was taught before the Buddha left, in his later years. The Buddha said, I don't talk about this with ordinary people who do not have wisdom. Those dummies just don't have enough wisdom. If I told them, they would think that there is a driving force out in the universe which is the originator of life. They would regard something without a self as having a self. Their consciousness will create a separation once again, and grasp onto an idea of the origin of life.

Life does not have an origin, it is just a flow phenomena, like the wind. Where can you say the wind comes from? If you say it came from the northwest, how about before the northwest? Beyond that it is empty. The Diamond Sutra tells you that all phenomena "arise from nowhere, and return to nowhere." Existence is emptiness and emptiness is existence. The Buddha taught this scientific principle, and everyone treated it as an existent whole. This is wrong. That's why the Buddha said, "Fearing that they would imagine and cling to it as to a self," so he dared not say it.

The seeds in this Alaya Consciousness are equal-flowing, but at the same time as this "equal-flow" is happening, "different-ripening (vipaka)," which is the law of cause and effect, is also happening. Every sentient being has good, bad, and neutral seeds. For example, everyone likes to be lazy, likes to leave the world behind to meditate and do spiritual practice. They don't want to do things. That is neutral karma. The consequences of neutral karma are very serious, so I point out to everyone that karma is very terrible. Human life comes from the transformations of "equal-flow" and "different-ripening." Ripening like when a fruit is ripe.

As for becoming a human, becoming a man or woman, becoming a dumb person or a smart person, becoming a good person or a bad person, these are all "different-ripening." If we take apples from Shandong to plant in the United States. Their taste will completely change. Also, the apples grow much bigger, completely different. In growing vegetables, fruits, and trees, there is a method called "grafting." When one tree is grafted to another, the taste and appearance of the fruit changes. This is also different ripening within karma.

Alaya Consciousness has "equal-flow" and "different-ripening." The Lankavatara Sutra tells us that some people are, by nature, just ordinary people and do not want to practice spirituality. Some people are spiritual by nature. Some love to practice the Hinayana, and are only interested in the Hearers path of liberation; some want to follow the path of the Mahayana Bodhisattva and eventually become a Buddha. He said that the differences in foundation [physical body] and receptive capacity are the karmic results of different-ripening. This is also called "foundation roots" and "seed natures." The Lankavatara Sutra does not use foundation roots, but rather, seed natures. For example, his surname is Wang, and her surname is Li, each family is different. This person has karmic seeds of Hinayana, that person has karmic seeds of Mahayana, this one has artistic seeds, that one has warrior or soldier seeds... Seed nature is the accumulated karma of many lifetimes, and belongs to "different-ripening."

"Ignorance is a condition for volition." If we look at this in reverse, where does this moment-by-moment ignorance come from? It is the power of life, like a waterfall, like flowing water, churning day and night. When we turn on a light, it looks like the light doesn't move, but in fact it's moving all the time. It's just that we can't see how the electricity connects to the light. This is ignorance. We only see the light shining continuously. In fact, every particle of it is in a constant state of transformation. From the perspective of different-ripening, the science of life is so subtle.

The twelve links of interdependent arising, can be understood in different ways. The monks of old had a solid foundation in fundamental studies and therefore were able to explain Buddhism very well. Nowadays, generally people who study Buddhism are not well versed in ordinary knowledge. In this era, it is useless to merely be well versed in ancient prose, you really also need to know about modern science. Buddhism is so deep!

Going back to the twelve causes and conditions, ignorance is a condition for volition. This moment-by-moment ignorance causes the power of life to continually move. Contained within this are equal-flow and different-ripening, although in this movement, there is a unity of mind and matter. You have to know that the physical world is always in motion, and ignorance also includes the unity of mind and matter. The skandha of volition is both mind and matter flowing together! Equal flow!

Now, since we are talking about the source of human life, I wanted to specifically draw upon the twelve links. Avija, no light, is ignorance and " no light " represents the functioning of ignorance within one's nature. The skandha of volition (行 xing— movement or action) is connected with the seventh consciousness, the root consciousness (manasvijnana). As to the Buddhist terms, mind (alayavijnana), root consciousness (manasvijnana), and consciousness (manovijnana), mind (alayavijnana) represents the origin of mind and matter. The root consciousness (manasvijnana) is the seventh consciousness which is the root of self-grasping and dharma-grasping. The consciousness that can think, imagine, distinguish and analyze is called the sixth consciousness (manovijnana). The root of this consciousness is the seventh consciousness (manasvijnana). These are the "mind, root consciousness and consciousness."

People often talk about Chan (Zen) nowadays. The Chan masters of old had a teaching method, we call it the bluffing method, tricking you saying, "Seek the answer outside of the mind, root consciousness and consciousness, seek!" If you leave your mind and consciousness, what seeking can be done! If you are able to do this, you have become an enlightened Buddha and you should not be seeking. They just used this feigning as a method of teaching. "Seek the answer outside of the mind, root consciousness and consciousness, go seek!" Nowadays, many people say this casually, but don't understand it. If you understand outside of the mind, root consciousness and consciousness, you are already there, no ignorance, no more movement of the volition skandha, you have become a Buddha. If I have become a Buddha, do I still need to go to your meditation hall? Humph!

The meditation hall is also called the seeking hall. When you go in there, you need to seek. When you go in, it is not to sit there forever holding tightly to something. What is that all about? What kind of karma is that creating! Well it can actually be considered good karma. In the next life, become a scholar, the only scholar in your world, however.

"Ignorance is a condition for volition. Volition is a condition for consciousness." This "consciousness" is the thinking consciousness, and it is divided into yin and yang. Because the driving force of volition is yang, the ling-hun is cognizant and clear. The active power of yang gives rise to all kinds of thought. The Consciousness Only School expands the parameters of the "consciousness" part of the twelve links of interdependent arising specifically, understanding the noumenon through all phenomena. Therefore it is called a Dharmalaksana (*dharma* meaning phenomena and *laksana* meaning characteristic, mark, or sign) school of thought.

The opposite of Dharmalaksana is Prajna. For example, the

Diamond Sutra is a Fundamental Nature school. It does not talk about appearance, covering up the view of phenomenon, overthrowing all phenomena, and directly turning the original nature of ignorance (ignorance=no light) into en*light*ened nature. which is the Prajna. This is the Fundamental Nature school, direct, and Chan/Zen uses the Fundamental Nature method.

The Consciousness-only approach follows along scientific lines, thoroughly studying the phenomenon, and finally returning to Fundamental Nature, Prajna, Original Nature.

Both Chan and Tantric Mahamudra first follow the line of Fundamental Nature. After enlightenment, they will have thousands of enlightenments understanding all of this phenomena, understanding everything, knowing everything is the great enlightenment of the Buddha. If you still aren't clear, don't understand, then you don't even understand the principles of the Buddhist scriptures. You will only grasp onto the "fragrant board"[7] like it was Buddha, or hold onto the bell, jingling it, reciting mantras as if this was Buddha. None of them. That's just a convenient door for ordinary people to find a direction to walk. Ordinary people like to grab something, so grab something for him to play with.

---

[7] The "fragrant board" is held by the person who is in charge of the meditation hall at a Chan temple.

The Buddha said in the Prajna Sutras that 'I have not spoken a word in 49 years. Do not think that I have taught the Dharma, no!' The Buddha said in the Lotus Sutra that there is only one path in Buddhism. Talking about 'east' talking about 'west' is merely an "empty fist to pacify a child." That is a teaching method to help you really understand the Suchness of the original nature. It's like when a child is crying, the adult makes a fist and says "don't cry, don't cry, I have candy for you." The child stops crying, and the adult opened his fist and, surprise, no candy, hey! It's an "empty fist to pacify a child". This is also called the "yellow leaf to pacify the child." A child is crying and won't stop but if you take a yellow leaf and say, "This is so beautiful! It's gold! If you don't cry, I will give you the gold. But if you cry again, I won't give it to you." The child says, "I want it, I won't cry." In the end, it is only a yellow leaf, this is the famous "yellow leaf to pacify the child."

When I went to a temple in Sichuan, I saw a couplet hanging there:

"Distant, distant mountains; babbling, babbling water; white cloud, cloud, urge the calf to return.

The wind is free, free; the rain is easy, easy; flutter, flutter, yellow leaf quells the crying child."

This is a wonderful couplet with talented calligraphy. Who

wrote this? It was composed and written by Zen Master Poshan Haiming. I saw the calligraphy of the ancient master Chen Tuan who wrote, "*A horse opens a swarth along the shore of the sky; A dragon among men wondrously escapes.*" I have seen calligraphy written by Zhang Sanfeng, and have seen calligraphy written by Master Poshan. I never again studied other calligraphy styles. The calligraphy of those accomplished Taoists and Buddhists are really extraordinary! This calligraphy couplet was also excellent, but unfortunately it is gone now.

"Distant, distant mountains; babbling, babbling water; white cloud, cloud, urge the calf to return." This is the education of Buddhism. Every method is to guide you back home and become a Buddha. The calf was running around, pulling the cow back, pulling this thought back, and returning to the bright and pure original nature. "The wind is free, free; the rain is easy, easy; flutter, flutter, yellow leaf quells the crying child." These lines are so well written! Master Poshan was truly enlightened.

Zhang Xianzhong arrived in Sichuan with a trail of dead bodies left in his wake. Therefore, Master Poshan wanted to meet with Zhang Xianzhong. Among the Master's disciples, the greatest Dharma protector was Qin Liangyu, a famous female general in Sichuan. She confronted Zhang Xianzhong in eastern Sichuan, in the area which is now Chongqing. Zhang Xianzhong had killed too many people in Eastern Sichuan. Master Poshan still insisted on meeting him. Qin Liangyu said, "No, Master, you are a monk, he will kill you." Master Po Shanming said that even if he tries to kill me, I will meet him and urge him not to kill. In the end, the Master went alone. As soon as Zhang Xianzhong saw him, he said "You came! Very good! What do you want, O'great monk?" The Master said, "Don't kill people!" Zhang Xianzhong said, "I can do that but on one condition, if you eat meat, I will not kill." Master Po Shan Ming said, "Bring me some meat!" He ate it on the spot, and Zhang Xianzhong said, "I will not kill."

Zen Master Poshan Haiming, at the age of 23, lived in Huangmei Potou Mountain for three years in order to realize the Tao. During the three years, he tried his best and still did not realize the Tao. Finally, he decided to give himself one last push to achieve realization within seven days. Four or five days later, the energy channels of his legs opened more and he walked as if floating in the clouds. He was not afraid nor did he make a big deal of it. But he was not yet enlightened. With that, he threw down the gauntlet and stood on the edge of a cliff and said, "Without enlightenment, life ends today." If I don't understand it today, let me die! After that, he entered a state where both he and his surroundings melted into oneness and nothingness. Then he saw flat ground in front of him, there was no cliff at all. He lifted his foot to take a step, to do walking meditation. In reality, he stepped over the edge and fell down the cliff. He broke his foot and became a cripple. After all, a cliff is still a cliff.

He later became enlightened and built Shuanggui Hall in what is now Chongqing, which I visited. He composed that couplet, and also did the calligraphy. Seeing that couplet...ah! Those of us who love literature cannot produce something of that caliber. His calligraphy was so free and easy! Very impressive! This was an eminent monk. It's not the empty, chaotic calligraphy people do now.

What is this topic I am talking about now? It is consciousness. Why are we talking about consciousness here? We went from consciousness to the Consciousness Only school, to the Fundamental Nature school and the Dharmalaksana school, they are all convenient means to help you realize your enlightenment.

Speaking of Consciousness Only *Vijñapti-mātra*, I said that in general books on Consciousness Only are correct, but they didn't recognize that the Consciousness Only *Vijñapti-mātra* is a specifically a guide for spiritual cultivation which helps you clearly understand any aspect or realm of experience. Nowadays everyone does not study it from this perspective. Instead, they have turned Consciousness Only into a philosophical thought. What does that have to do with cultivation?

Ignorance is a condition for volition. Volition is a condition for consciousness. This consciousness, in terms of life, is the *ling-hun*. How does this ling-hun integrate with the body? How does thought arise within this body of flesh? How do they come together and become a life? So "Consciousness is a condition for name and form" is more difficult to understand.

In old times, sperm and egg cell were called father's essence and mother's blood. In fact, if you really talk about essence, what is essence? We say that men produce sperm, and women produce water when they have sex. These are both "essence." However, the Buddha made it very clear that essence is spread throughout the whole body, and the "essence" that comes out from there is already discarded waste material. The whole body is essence, that is, every cell and every place in the body is essence. Moreover, in the Buddhist scriptures, the Vinaya tells us that the essence of men is generally divided into seven categories: "cyan, yellow, red, white, black, cream, and buttermilk." Cyan is the essence of a wheel-turning king; yellow is the essence of the princes of a wheel-turning king (chakravartin); red is the essence of excessive play with female sex; white is the essence of ordinary people; black is the essence of the minister of a wheel-turning king; cream color is essence of a Stream-enterer (*sotāpanna* (Pali), *śrotāpanna* (Sanskrit)); buttermilk color is the essence of once-returner (*Sakadāgāmin* (Pali), *Sakṛdāgāmin* (Sanskrit)).

Then, when the man and woman ejaculate, the sperm and

egg come together. The bardo person is stirred by karma and there is a strong suction. It gets sucked in and mixes with the fertilized egg. This mixture of heartmind and physical form is called "name and form."

When you first sit down to meditate, your state of mind is quite pure. Why do you lose that purity soon after? The suction of the mind begins again, sucking in distractions from the outside world. You can't let go. In Chan/Zen they say—let go! You can't let go, you suck everything inward. This is the second of the Four Noble Truths, the origin of suffering, gathering (*taṇhā*, lit. "thirst"). We are gathering anytime and anywhere, grasping thoughts, grasping feelings, grasping everything.

"Name" (*nama*) belongs to the concept of spirit, thought, volition and consciousness belong to the scope of name. *Nama* has no visible form. The soul of the bardo body is spiritual and belongs to the scope of the name.

What is "form" (*rupa*)? The elements of earth, water, fire and wind, material form is called *rupa*. Sperm and ovum are physiological and material. The four great elements belong to the scope of "*rupa*".

The combination of sperm and ovum coupled with your soul, when these three things come together "wham," you can't get out of that powerful suction. This is reincarnation, you get sucked in and take rebirth. This is called "name and form, *namarupa*."

The "*namarupa*" changes every seven days. For the first seven days, it was sparse. The Buddhist scriptures describe it as congealed milk, like the jelly children eat now. One change every seven days, slowly growing. But your consciousness, your spirit, your heart, and your mental consciousness can't jump out of this volitional force. You can't get out of it, and this is what is called reincarnation, revolving in this cycle forever. Like a fly caught in an electric fan, as long as the electric fan is on, the fly cannot get out. It can only fly out when the electric fan is turned off. Our thinking minds and ling-huns, all the karmic fruits brought about by our previous lives, are wrapped up in this *namarupa*, name and form.

This *namarupa* has an obvious growth pattern every seven days. For details, please refer to the "The Teaching to Venerable Nanda on Entry into the Womb" (Āyuṣmannandagarbhāvakrāntinirdeśa) which was spoken by the Buddha more than two thousand years ago, and is very detailed. Modern medicine provides some evidence to prove that the Buddha was correct. After studying the "The Teaching to Venerable Nanda on Entry into the Womb," you will understand that if you sit there and meditate for seven hours, seven minutes, seven seconds, or seven days, there is a change. It is the same principle that operates in fetal growth. But if you don't practice, what's the use of calling me Teacher! You are all fooling yourselves.

"*Namarupa* is a condition of the six sense bases[8] (Pali-*saḷāyatana* Sanskrit- *ṣaḍāyatana*))." What are the "six entrances/sense bases"? The eyes, ears, nose, tongue, body and consciousness are called the six sense roots, which are inherent in name and form. Sights, sounds, fragrances, tastes, touch, and mental phenomena are called the six sense objects[9], which are objects in the physical and mental world. Because the six sense objects enter into the six sense roots, hence the name, "six entrances."

When I first read Buddhist scriptures, and saw that in relation to the six roots and six kinds of dust, I wondered why use the word "入" enter/ entrance here? Strange! So I just paid attention. Earlier, I asked you to pay attention to the ten categories of "all entries," earth, water, fire, wind, cyan, yellow, crimson, white, emptiness, and consciousness. "All entries" refers to all the things which permeate us. For example, we are sitting in this room, how do you feel? The weather today is a

---

[8] In Chinese, the term *saḷāyatana* is translated as the six "entrances" and not sense bases.
[9] In Chinese, they are called the "six kinds of dust."

little more stuffy than yesterday, isn't it? The humidity is high, it permeates us and you can't stand it.

Did you think that since the room is closed, the external environment cannot be felt? It seeps in. We just use heaters to adjust the room, otherwise everyone will not be so comfortable sitting here. Through this you can understand that the physical environment and mental environment from the outside permeate your body and mind. Sights, sounds, fragrances, tastes, touch, and mental phenomena seep into and make contact with you, so they are called the "Six Entrances."

You need to study Theravada Buddhist sutras. Buddhist scriptures are very scientific. There are ten categories of "all entries." The five elements of earth, water, fire, wind and emptiness, plus consciousness which functions in the realms of the rational, conceptual, and the spiritual. Cyan, yellow, crimson and white are phenomena that occur when physical elements of earth, water, fire, and wind transform. No matter where you are, in any region, they permeate you.

As you look into this, you find that there is no "black," right? Why? Reading Buddhist scriptures should be like doing scientific research. Buddha said cyan, yellow, crimson and white. Why did he forget black? He has not forgotten. There is actually no black, the combination of all colors is black. There are many colors.

For example, when you were in middle school, you were taught seven colors: red, orange, yellow, green, blue, indigo, and purple, right? Not only seven, many more colors can be created. After all colors are combined, it becomes black. White reflects all colors. All colors are created, and this is all part of physical sciences. So if you don't understand science, don't talk about spiritual practice. In ancient times, those masters who had obtained the Dao understood, but their ways of expression were different.

Knowing about ten types of entry, you will understand why you can't just sit there steadily. You are affected by external influences such as weather, earth, water, fire, wind, and emptiness, and even various phenomena and realms, which can change and stimulate you at any time. If your mind power is not strong and your wisdom is not enough, you will grab onto these. You can't ignore them. So the Prajna school talks about emptiness, telling you to dissipate everything and let go. But what do people do? Their habit is to grasp. This life, at the time of entering the womb, when consciousness provided the condition for name and form to arise, you got sucked in. But can you really hold fast to what you grasp? You can't hold on. Just as when you inhale and try to hold, it will disperse. The more intensely you try to gather and hold on, the more it loosens and disperses, the greater is the reactive force. This is the same in psychology, physiology, and mechanics.

The twelve interdependent links of causation, ignorance is a condition for consciousness. Consciousness is a condition for name and form. Name and form are conditions for the six sense bases. The six sense bases are conditions for contact. We have discussed up to "contact." When there are six entrances, contact occurs. Contact is an exchange, an exchange of feelings and mutual influence.

"Contact is a condition for feeling." When there is contact, feelings occur. You said, I caught a cold when the wind blew on me. That is from the "ten categories of all entries," from within the four elements of "earth, water, fire, wind." The wind came in, or the air-conditioner came in and you caught a cold. After catching cold, inflammation began inside, the "fire" started. Your nose was runny and then your nose became blocked. The water element became severely blocked. The elements of earth, water, fire, and wind change inside. There was too much contact and feeling.

From the day we were born from our mother to the present, there has no been one day that has been comfortable. Every second of contact and feeling is very painful. But people don't feel it because they are numb, they are used to it, and they do not have enough wisdom to observe clearly. Once you can leave contact and feeling, you will become a body of rainbow light, a field light, ethereal and one with the void. That is the meditative state of boundless space. This is not a theory, nor an illusion, but an actual result.

The key to this intermediate practice is to rely on the power of your mind to not be driven by this karma. So I ask you to understand the "Thirty-seven Factors of Enlightenment (Bodhipaksa)" very carefully. Meditating is just to practice learning concentration! You can be calm while sitting, but you have to be able to be calm at any time while walking, sitting, sitting, and lying. If even the root of concentration is not well established, if among the five roots there is no root of concentration, of course there will be no power of concentration. How could you not be driven by karma? The five roots are the root of faith, the root of diligence, the root of mindfulness, the root of concentration, and the root of wisdom. Based on the five roots, the five powers of faith, effort, mindfulness, concentration, and wisdom are initiated. With the power of wisdom, when wisdom becomes power, it breaks all attachments, and that is called cultivation.

Contact and feeling are very tough to deal with, all sentient beings are deceived by feeling. Why do men and women have sex? It feels comfortable to be touched in that way! But it is short-lived. Because of this contact, feelings arise which you call enjoyment. Look, when you reach sexual orgasm, it is gone in less than a minute and all the power dissipates. As the climax begins, the ten categories of entries all enter and start to conglomerate. That power gets concentrated, explodes, and disperses again. In the end, there is nothing. But ordinary beings are foolish, without wisdom, and deceived by all this. Therefore, feeling is the feeling.

"Feeling is a condition for craving." Craving means to like and covet. "Craving is a condition for grasping." Grasping means you want to grasp onto things you can't be grasped. So I said you desperately grasp wealth, power, and high positions. What is the use? Those are temporary possessions, there for you to use for a while. They are not yours, and will disperse.

"Grasping is a condition for becoming." You have something in hand, but this so-called possession is temporary. It 'belongs' to you, but it does not really belong to you. You have been fooled, everything will change and disappear. Even if you use up part of it, and it seems then that the part that you used really belongs to you, you are still fooling yourself. It is merely a momentary gathering of conditions from which contact and feelings arise.

Everything is but the gathering of causes and conditions and then their dissolution and dispersal. There is no "acquiring" at all, you have never really possessed anything. Even your own body and mind are in a process of metabolic transformation at all times, unceasing. The so-called gains and possessions are just ideas, self deceptive thoughts. Since there is no gain, of course there is nothing to lose. If you really see this truth clearly, you won't be desperately trying to grasp, and you will be able to contribute unreservedly to society. This is called doing no evil, practicing all virtues and purifying the mind. It's not an intentional effort to be good, it's natural. Of course, we need to do this wisely, not chaotically.

"Becoming is a condition for rebirth. Rebirth is a condition for old age and death." Because of "becoming," there is pregnancy and rebirth and then aging and death. Life is like this, whether it be an event or a physical object, all composite things are like this. What comes into being must finally come to an end or to destruction.

After old age is death, the *ling-hun* will come again, and ignorance is a condition for volition... just like this rebirth continues. This is a general principle. Only after understanding this can we understand how rebirth comes about, what life is about. Get the picture?

Now it's time to get ready to eat. You see, I have expended so much energy to teach you. You have been with me for many years, and you have still not understood. What use is it! This is a *huatou*! In the meditation hall, everything is a *huatou*, so go and pierce through!

For example, when you meditate, sometimes the pain is unbearable. You have to know that "feeling is emptiness." No matter how painful, you cannot retain the pain, it's impermanent! The impermanence of all action is the natural law of arising and cessation; arising from nowhere and returning to nowhere. Coming from emptiness and returning to emptiness. It is as if something has come, don't be fooled by it. Don't you recite the Heart Sutra? The Heart Sutra tells you that "Form is emptiness, emptiness is form. Form is not other than emptiness, and emptiness is not other than form." Then you must know that when you are sad, you will say "Feeling is emptiness, emptiness is feeling. Feeling is not other than emptiness, emptiness is not other than feeling!" If you have more thoughts, know that "thinking is emptiness, emptiness is thinking. Thinking is not other than empty, and emptiness is not other than thinking." Regardless of whether you are a monk or studying Buddhism as a lay person, what are you learning! Trapped by your own feelings, smothering there! It's the skandha of feeling. You were deceived by it. Sometimes, you might feel quite comfortable. It is because skandhas of feeling and thinking are in accord. And you mistakenly think that this is samādhi! Goddammit!

Session Six

The twelve sufferings within life

Striving toward no suffering

Where is the Dharmakaya

How is a fetus formed

The whirling of habit energy

Growth of a baby in the womb

The realm of a baby in the womb

● The retribution for suicide

Entering, living in, and exiting the womb consciously

Heavenly realms

Transforming the Four Great Elements through the element of wind

Everyone knows all about Theravada but if I tested you on the Four Noble Truths, the twelve links of dependent arising, some of you would fail. Especially these lay Buddhists who like talking about Buddhism, they just want to be part of the action and have fun. These lay Buddhists do meditation because they want to play with supernatural powers, get healthy, entertain themselves, play around with the Dharma. They just want a little profit, like doing business, but they don't really want to learn Buddhism.

When Buddha taught Dharma for the first time, he talked about the Four Noble Truths. The so-called Hinayana is like elementary school, and Mahayana is like university. Hinayana is basic education. Some people have not learned a basic education, but they talk about Mahayana. They talk about Chan, Tantra, and Yogacara. They are all deceiving themselves and others.

The Four Noble Truths are suffering, the cause of suffering, the cessation of suffering and the path to the cessation of suffering. I also often ask these monks, in the Buddhist scriptures it says that the Buddha turned the wheel of Dharma of the Four Noble Truths three times, how can it be turned three times? It means to talk about how ignorance is a condition for volition, volition is a condition for consciousness... to enlighten everyone that all life in this world and the physical world itself, everything is suffering and there is no real happiness. Except for what Mr. Xu described earlier, it was very comfortable when his soul left the body. He felt very happy and is still nostalgic about that experience. In fact, everything in this world is suffering, and so there are eight or twelve categories of suffering.

If I question you lay people, can you recite them? The eight sufferings are birth, old age, sickness, and death, not getting what you wish for, separation from that which you love, meeting with something you can't stand, and the "blazing" five skandhas. You carefully read a lot of Buddhist scriptures, each scripture only talks about one type of suffering but from this you can extrapolate many, many others. The eight sufferings are the larger fundamentals which summarize the most painful things in life. You won't understand them through memorization. In fact, sociology, economics, political science, pedagogy... are all connected with them.

Ordinarily speaking eight sufferings, there are twelve sufferings when speaking profoundly, and the eight sufferings plus the four sufferings of worry, sorrow, anxiety, and frustration are the twelve principles. In other words, human life is full of pain and suffering.

You ask me the question about life, and I usually tell you that there are three things which describe human life: We mysteriously take birth, reluctantly live on and then die inexplicably. Everyone is like this, they mysteriously take birth and don't know how they came here or why they were born. And life? Reluctantly live on, you pursue this and that, or as you always say, in pursuit of happiness and good fortune. So it is obvious that you are all unhappy or unfortunate. Not wanting to die, but life is such suffering, just living on like this. Finally death comes, and you leave without knowing why. That's the story. Therefore, the Buddha said that everything is suffering.

How does the Buddha explain suffering? Common scholars say that the Buddha's view of society, life, and the world is pessimistic. This is what philosophers say. The Buddha only tells you that everyone is living in suffering like this. He doesn't say that our original state is suffering. He has a method to jump out of this suffering and to obtain bliss which he teaches us how to practice. This is the purpose of the Buddha.

He sighs and tells us that there is suffering in the world, so that we can understand the world and all of human society. All in all, life is suffering, but there is something which is not suffering, go and seek it. This is the purpose of the Buddha, to become liberated and find bliss without suffering. It is called Sukavati, the realm of bliss. Sukavati is not only the world of Amitabha Buddha. Any realm of complete liberation from suffering with only happiness is a world of bliss.

Yesterday, Hu Songnian asked about "jumping out of the Three Realms," where does one jump to? I also often ask everyone, your cultivation practice says to "jump out of the three realms; not within the five elements." Where do you go outside the three realms? Is there a fourth realm? The Buddha did not say. Not in the five elements, where is it? Is it in the sixth one? No one answers, but you need to find out.

Indeed, the Buddha said to jump out of the Three Realms, but jump to which realm? Yes, the Dharma Realm. Didn't the Buddha tell you? That's not a fourth realm, it's in the three realms, but it transcends them. The Buddha gave it a name, the Dharma Realm which transcends time and space. You only know how to talk about suffering, you take it in very pessimistically, and think that religion is pessimistic. You need to know, the Buddha started from suffering, but the highest goal is to become liberated from suffering and attain bliss.

Back when I was young, I taught philosophy at Sichuan University. I would ask everyone, what is the general purpose of life? No one could answer. In the end, I would tell everyone that the aim is to get away from suffering and attain happiness. All sentient beings want to get out of suffering; not only people, but any bacteria and insects, want to get out and find bliss. The Dharma Realm is bliss. Buddhism has a standard and that is bliss.

What is meant by "samudaya," the second Noble Truth? Suffering was accumulated by yourself, it was gathered by yourself. For example, if you want money to do business, accumulating all the money for yourself is a form of suffering. And once you have accumulated it all, you really suffer even more. So gathering is the cause of suffering. I just spoke about the twelve links, where is the accumulating? "Craving and grasping," to crave, to grasp, to possess. From beginningless time, craving, grasping, and then losing everything. Nothing can be held onto, it all disperses. You should know that right now you are grasping, grasping your thoughts, grasping your feelings, and you are all deceived by these. So craving and grasping is the cause of suffering. You gather dollar after dollar, bit by bit gathering it. Scholar and intellectuals, from kindergarten to university, to doctoral degree, accumulate knowledge. The more knowledge, the greater the suffering. When there is accumulation there is suffering, accumulation is the cause of suffering. What is "suffering"? Suffering is nothing but the fruit of collection. The Four Noble Truths starts with the result, suffering, so that you can understand the cause of suffering.

What are "Cessation" and "Path," in the Four Noble Truths? Cessation means having let go of everything, having nothing, emptiness. How can I empty everything? Only when your wisdom understands it, can you be empty. The "Way" (Dao) is the cause of cessation. Gaining the Dao, wisdom is accomplished, and all the causes of suffering are eliminated. Attaining this Dao can eliminate all suffering. With no suffering at all, there is bliss.

This is the first turning of the Dharma wheel of the Four Noble Truths. In Chan, you are asked to seek the origin. This is called Huatou, the Huatou is the question, the problem. If you don't study the problem yourself, what kind of Buddhist student are you?

What is the second turning of the Dharma wheel of the Four Noble Truths? The twelve interdependent links of arising which we just analyzed, do you remember it all? In China, we have turned it into a four-sentence verse. I often tell you to recite it:

Ignorance, craving, and grasping are three defilements;
Volition and becoming refer to karma;
From consciousness to contact, plus birth and death;
These seven have a single name, the fruit of suffering.

"Ignorance, craving, and grasping are three defilements." Within the twelve links, ignorance, craving, and grasping, these three are the fundamental defilements. Within the Four Noble Truths, they are the accumulation of suffering. As soon as the moment by moment ignorance arises, the unclear mind wants to grasp hold of what it craves and hold onto it forever. Thus there is great suffering. These three are the roots of troubles and suffering.

"Volition and becoming refer to karma." Ignorance is a condition for volition. Volition is the original driving force. Within the Twelve Links, the tenth is becoming, all from grasping. Volition and becoming are the force of karma. This driving force of life has been there life after life in the past up to now and on into the future lives. This momentum, this force, all full of turmoil, is within the volition. Deceived by the illusions of having made a name for oneself, having wealth, having children and grandchildren, having love, having family, illness...all illusions. There are two branches of volition. Actually, the three basic forces within volition are ignorance, craving, and grasping. Because of karma, ignorance, craving, and grasping arise. From this accumulation comes suffering and because of ignorance, craving, and grasping, you are always in volitional action, always grasping. Everything must be possessed, all attachments, and everything that belongs to oneself must be grasped. This is what is called karma.

"From consciousness to contact, plus birth and death, these seven have a single name, the fruit of suffering." The functions of life, death and rebirth, and again life and death of the body start from the mind and consciousness. It's the consciousness that comes into the womb. The spirit combines with the great elements of the earth, fire, water and wind to form the body's physical cells. From consciousness to *namarupa* (name and form), to the six entrances, to contact, to feeling, then rebirth, and aging and death, these seven links are the fruits of suffering. This is the second turning of the Four Noble Truths.

This so-called turning means to analyze and show. Look at the scientific logic of Buddha, it's very thorough, and it's analyzed very clearly for you.

Just now, after we ate, a classmate told me the truth. I asked him if he was tired of listening? He said I'm not tired but, Teacher, you are tired! I can only laugh. I asked him what he thought of the talks. He said that there were many things he did not understand. I didn't say anything. Hehe! I couldn't deny what he said, nor affirm it. He was right. If he fully understood it, that would be astonishing. He said honestly that he partly understood, but most of it, he really didn't really understand. You other classmates, all of you pretend to understand very well, but in fact none of you understand. He is telling the truth. Most people are not honest, and they say that they understand. Who understands? On the other hand, if you really understood clearly, that's a different story, that would be incredible.

""Ignorance, craving, and grasping are three defilements. Volition and becoming refer to karma. From consciousness to contact, plus birth and death, these seven have a single name, the fruit of suffering." Memorize these four sentences. Why memorize them? The hard work in meditation is just this. As you break through this bit by bit, your skill and wisdom will advance step by step. Don't just sit for a few hours like a fool. I ask you, what good would it do for you to sit there for a hundred years? Does sitting mean Tao? If you sit down for a hundred years, you are not as good as that stone monkey or stone lion, right? It can sit for hundreds of years without moving. Has it gained the Tao?

So Taoist Zhang Ziyang has two poems about meditation practice, "If there are no real seeds in the abdominal cauldron, it is like trying to cook with nothing but water in the pot." Sitting here, if you don't have a bit of the real thing in your heartmind, it is like the pot with nothing but water. Even after 10,000 years of cooking, you won't be able to produce the pill of immortality (*dan*). So Taoists call this, "alchemy" (*lien dan*). The word "*dan*" 丹 has a point in the middle, a central point, but you don't! So in the Chan meditation hall, you are asked to hold onto a *huatou*, hold onto mindfulness. If you don't, then you don't have that point inside and there is no true seed. In that case, what is the use? Sitting for a few hours, sitting for dozens of days, no matter how many years, it is useless!

I'm not explaining theory to you right now. If you have experiential understanding of this then you are on the path of actual practice. I have told you the main points. But do you understand? I don't know. It is my business whether I tell you or not. It's your business whether you understand or not.

Let's return to talking about taking rebirth (lit. entering the womb). If you have understood the Four Noble Truths and the Twelve Links of Interdependent Origination, then you will know how rebirth happens, you will know how to meditate and what to work on.

Just earlier, I talked about entering the womb. What the Buddha said is that the three conditions are needed in combination for pregnancy to occur and to become a new life. This is the different ripening of karmic fruit of the alayavijnana, and the karma matures to become a human being.

Let me first declare that this is talking about normal human rebirth, and not about the six paths of rebirth, so don't be mistaken. When the male sperm and the female egg come into contact with each other, pregnancy doesn't necessarily result. It won't work without a bardo being. However, even if a bardo being enters, complications might occur, for example an ectopic pregnancy, and a fetus will not be able to form.

It is difficult to become a human. There are a lot of things regarding this in the Buddhist scriptures. Whether it be the "The

Teaching to Venerable Nanda on Entry into the Womb" or any other sutra on this subject, the Buddha spoke these thousands of years ago and they stand up to comparison with modern medicine. The Buddha said that there are many conditions regarding the female uterus. If the uterus is too long, too short, or too posterior, it is not easy to get pregnant. Sometimes, the uterus may be too cold, or too hot to get pregnant. Some types of venereal diseases or other diseases may preclude women from getting pregnant. Even if women are healthy, there are dozens of conditions which would inhibit pregnancy.

I ask you, 2,600 years ago, India was not so advanced in medical science. How was Buddha Shakyamuni able to talk about it so clearly? Modern medicine has not exceeded his scope.

Then in regards to men, if the sperm is unhealthy, pregnancy cannot be achieved. Too cold, too hot, too hungry, or even bad moods will cause leakage. There is also a lot of knowledge about sexual disorders in the Buddhist sutras. If you really study Buddhism and write a book about sexual relations and disorders, you could write several PhDs. But as for all of you, you are not learned, don't read books, don't read sutras.

I often tell young students not to go out and fool around. Do you think no one knows? When the two of you are having sex there, hundreds of millions of bardo beings are watching.

They're looking for an opportunity to enter the womb and reincarnate.

How many sperm does a man send out at one time? 600 million to 1.2 billion. I asked medical scientists whether there is metabolism in the male spermatozoa. A gynecologist answered, probably yes. Then there are tens of thousands of women's eggs, and they can only discharge 400 to 500 eggs in their lifetime. If they cannot be discharged, do they become something else in the body? If they stay in the body, they need to be transforming all the time. If they cannot transform, is the body healthy or unhealthy? This is a big medical health issue, not that simple.

Today we formally say that Buddhism studies life science and cognitive science. Knowing and understanding life, you will understand ignorance, know and understand yourself. In science, this is the direction that is being explored now, called cognitive science. Foreign countries have just started. They don't know that Chinese Buddhism has been talking about this for many, many years. But people who study Buddhism, both monks and lay practitioners, do not know about cognitive or life science. The West is doing preliminary research, and our country has just begun. In fact, this already belonged to us, we have the greatest treasures but we just threw them into a pile of manure and buried that in the backyard. The culture of China, what is it? What is Chinese culture? Acting in a movie, painting a picture, and writing a few calligraphy characters, is this culture?

Well, this sperm and egg have combined, and the bardo being has entered the womb. We are talking about a normal human pregnancy. Well, the first seven days, as mentioned yesterday, the consistency is like jelly that children eat, a tiny little blob. But even here, the chi-energy of life is whirling at the same time. In Buddhism, this is called habit energy. Throughout many lives, many worlds, this habit energy has been revolving. This jelly-like thing, turning round and round in the mother's womb, changes every seven days. A central energy channel arises, which will later transform into the spinal column. It changes every seven days, and the wind of each seven days has a name in Buddhism. This wind is what the Chinese refer to as *qi/chi*, the power of movement. For a total of thirty-eight segments of seven days, a little more than nine months, the body grows. At the end of the pregnancy, the last wind, the inverting wind, the inverting power turns the baby's body upside down, preparing for a normal birth. I won't say much about this, you can study the details in the Buddha's "The Teaching to Venerable Nanda on Entry into the Womb"

In the mother's womb, a boy tends to face the mother's back bone, so in folk tradition people say that if a pregnant woman has a more pointy belly, she will give birth to a boy. This is because the backside of a male baby is pointed toward the mother's belly.

Female babies are the other way round, facing outward. This is why in folk tradition people say that if a pregnant woman's belly looks flat on the outside, the baby will be a girl. Many times I have mentioned that when people die in the water and float up, a male will float facing downward on his stomach, and a female floats facing upward on her back. This is just like the fetus in the womb.

The growth of the fetus is contingent upon this chi, this powerful movement of circulating energy. The Buddha, still speaking in simple terms, describes the changes in each seven day period. He tells which meridians grow in a certain seven day period to become a heart, a lung, a brain, an eye, an ear, and so on. Sometime during the middle of the third to fifth month, the fetus will become conscious in the womb and will become aware of the parents and environment outside. The baby can hear and know, but cannot differentiate. The baby also has joy, anger, sorrow, and happiness in the mother's womb. Similar to Mr. Xu's experience when he drank and lay forward on the table, and went floating around up there. A fetus also experiences this kind of state inside the womb. So sometimes pregnant women say that the baby is kicking around in her belly. The baby is not merely kicking, it is its own realm inside there and maybe is racing, playing sports, or doing martial arts, or maybe just trying to adjust its body position. In the same way, when you meditate, sometimes you experience some kind of realm. This is a science.

Then the Buddha described the normal circumstances when entering the womb. A thought of sexual desire arises in the bardo being. Seeing a man and a woman having sex, the bardo being will be attracted to those two who will become his parents. When the the bardo being approaches, the parents are no longer seen, only the two sex organs in motion. If he likes the woman, it's as if he becomes the man having sex with this woman. He is actually coming together with his mother, and he will be a male when he is born. If she likes the man, as if she were having sex with him. She is actually having sex with her father and becomes a female.

Freud knew this, so he believed that boys are subconsciously attracted to their mothers, and girls are subconsciously attracted to their fathers. Freud's psychology is sexual psychology. I repeat that he understood a little but not all.

Then, the Buddha once again tells you that human life is not easy to obtain. Some lives end early, dying in the womb. Why? Their karma is to die in the womb. Some are about to be born when their life karma is finished and some die during birth. Buddha gave many examples like this. It is hard to attain a human body and this life, this existence, is not easy. Therefore, Buddhism believes that suicide is an offense, and there are rule against committing suicide. Why do people commit suicide? They feel that life is very bitter, like a kind of punishment, and they want to get out earlier by committing suicide. Wrong, this will bring damnation upon damnation. You did not complete your original sentence. Committing suicide is like escaping from prison. If you escape, you will suffer more and more punishment. So suicide is not a way of relief.

Taking rebirth is not necessarily always because of sexual desire. Some beings, as I said just now, are fine in the mother's womb but then the karma of the life of their consciousness ends and they die in the womb. Another consciousness enters, that is, another bardo being enters. Some have just been born, but their consciousness dies, leaves the body, and another bardo being enters at this time. So it is not necessarily true that taking rebirth is because of sexual desire. There are other different situations. This is very complex, so go and read "The Teaching to Venerable Nanda on Entry into the Womb."

You asked the question of reincarnation without forgetting, like some of the reincarnated rinpoches, are they clear about their past lives? Very few, very rarely. The Buddha said that only great bodhisattvas and great arhats with very high concentration and wisdom can do it. According to the Buddhist scriptures, in general, arahants and bodhisattvas lose their memory entering into the womb, or while in the womb, or coming out of the womb. All of them become amnesic and everything from the previous life is forgotten and they become separated from their previous identity. This is called "The Veil of Separation." If you have a strong focus of concentration and you are not taking rebirth in a state of ignorance, you do not get sucked in, you enter the womb of your own initiative. Shakyamuni did not enter the womb out of ignorance. The second step is to stay in the womb without ignorance arising. Throughout the stages of development in the womb, you are still doing spiritual practice, you are still in the realm of Bodhi-mandala, and your right awareness has not diminished. The third step is to be born without the veil of separation. You are born knowing. You can remember past knowledge and your wisdom is very bright.

As for determining whose reincarnation a person is depending on divination, I don't know about that. Then I can also say, Hu Songnian, you are my daughter reincarnated! Someone else is the reincarnation of the garuda I had raised! People make all sorts of claims, all sorts of nonsense now!

This is what the Buddha said, unless you enter the womb without ignorance, stay in the womb without ignorance, and take birth without ignorance, you cannot be born knowing. What is meant by "without ignorance" is clarity. For example, the Buddha said that he has done everything in his life. Looking at the Buddhist scriptures, you can see that the Buddha has done everything. He has been a wild beast, a rabbit, a bird, and so on, and so have we as well. If you put together the stories of the Buddha's many past lives, it would make a great book to educate children.

Therefore, Buddhism says that all of us must have "compassion without conditions, and empathy as if sharing the same body." We are sitting together, who knows if we have been parents to each other in our previous lives! Some people may have been husband and wife, may have been their children. We have gone back and forth taking turns over and over again. Who actually knows who they are! Therefore, if you are not happy with this friend and want to hassle him, you may just be hassling your previous father, or child, or brother. Therefore, have "compassion without conditions, and empathy as if sharing the same body."

Buddhist sutras tell us that sometimes a person enters the womb without seeing the man and woman engaging in sex. He said if, in this life, the person is stingy and gives people a hard time, but the other aspects of their character are good, they will become a human in their next life but will be poor. Their bardo time is like a dream where they suddenly feel like they are in a typhoon with thunder, heavy rains. All wet and scared, they try to flee. At this time they see a thatched hut or a cave and quickly run in to hide. At this point, they have entered the womb without having seen the man and woman engaged in sex. They are born into a poor family and their life is very difficult.

Sometimes, the bardo being goes to a place which is windy and sunny, and has beautiful buildings. They go inside to play and are born into a rich family. Therefore, there are many reasons for entering the womb, and you may not necessarily see anyone having sex.

For example, Mr. Xu told us about the time he was tired and his hun-soul flew upward. If he had really died, he would have gone to a heaven realm, but not the highest heaven. There are twenty-eight levels within the three heavenly realms: the Desire Realm, the Form Realm, and the Formless Realm. What Mr. Xu and his friend Mr. Wang described was the lowest heaven in the Desire Realm, the Heaven of the Four Heavenly Kings which is close to this world, a little higher than us, and still in the solar system. Above the Four Kings Heaven is the Thirty-three Heaven[10]. Thirty-three Heaven is not 33 levels, it is organized like the United Nations. The King of Thirty-three Heaven in Chinese Taoism is called the Jade Emperor, and Buddhists call him Sakra Devanam, or Indra. This is still within the solar system.

Above the Thirty-three Heaven are Yama Heaven, Tushita

---

[10] *Trāyastriṃśa* त्रायस्त्रिंश (Sanskrit) or *Tāvatiṃsa* तावतिंस (Tibetan)

Heaven, Nirmanarati Heaven, and Parinirmita-Vasavartin Heaven. These are the heavens of the Desire Realm, with a total of six major levels. These heavenly beings cannot do without six objects of desire—color, sound, fragrance, and touch—so they are called the six desire heavens. There is another explanation for the six desires, which refers to sexual desire, desire for appearance, desire for prestige, desire for speech and voice, desire for smoothness, and desire for thoughts. In short, there are various desires both physically and mentally.

Male and female are distinct in the world of desire. Laughter, gazing, intercourse, hugging, and caressing—you see me, I see you, we laugh together, love, hug, touch, and have sexual relations. However, the higher the level of heaven, the more different the form of sexual relations. Some just hold each other's hands and the action is completed. Their level is higher than ours and more comfortable. One level higher, there is no need to even hold hands. The two of them smile at each other and it's finished. And the children in these heavens are not born from the underside of a woman but from a man, from the shoulders, or from the top of the head, or from the side of the leg, all kinds. It sounds like mythology, but it is all very clearly delineated.

You study Buddhism but you haven't studied these. What kind of Buddhism are you studying! You don't know what realm you have meditated to, or where you are close to reaching. You ask those masters, which realm is this experience from, and most teachers don't know.

Yama Heaven is also called the "heaven without fighting." Our earth's time is based on the solar system. The Yama Heaven is probably beyond this solar system, their time is different, relatively. In their world, one day and night are measured in the time it takes for one of their lotus flowers to open and close, which is equal to two hundred years here. Therefore, they look at humans like we humans look at mayflies. We are inferior to mayflies, people born in the morning will die before noon. They have no sun or moon, the heavenly beings shine by themselves. In their realm, sexual desires of men and women are satisfied by holding hands.

Above Yama Heaven is Tusita Heaven. Maitreya Bodhisattva dwells in the inner sanctum there teaching the Dharma. Outside of this sanctum, the six desires still exist. To satisfy desire, men and women just need to smile at each other. Imagine that we are now in Maitreya's inner sanctum, talking in this room. Outside, people are drinking alcohol, eating meat, and doing all sorts of unseemly things. One day in Tusita Heaven is equal to four hundred years here.

What is above Tusita Heaven? It's the Nirmanarati Heaven,

also known as the heaven of devas "delighting in their creations." One day is equal to our 800 years. The man and woman smiled, and the sex was completed. Children were born from the area of the male's knee. In their world, you can self-manifest all kinds of things to eat and play with. They have power of concentration, but it's not true samadhi. It is merely the meditative concentration of the Desire Realm. So, who is reborn in the Nirmanarati Heaven after dying? The Surangama Sutra describes them as those for whom "the taste of horizontal activity is the same as chewing wax." This is saying that if, for healthy men and women, having sex is no more exciting than chewing wax, that there is no joy at all, it means that their sexual desire is basically non-existent. Such people will be born in Nirmanarati Heaven after death. Of course, this must be accompanied by a lot of good deeds.

The heaven above Nirmanarati Heaven is called Parinirmita-Vasavartin Heaven. It is a heaven controlled by the Demon King Vaśavartin, who is the lord of the entire realm of desire. Before Buddha Shakyamuni attained complete enlightenment, he was the one who interfered with and tested Siddhartha beneath the Bodhi tree. In the Parinirmita-Vasavartin Heaven, men and women only need to gaze at each other, to complete the act of sex. Unlike Nirmanarati Heaven, they don't manifest things by themselves for entertainment. Rather, they steal the things which are manifested by the beings in the Nirmanarati Heaven. They go down to the Nirmanarati Heaven and trick people with illusions. When the people there are basking in happiness from the illusions, the things they themselves had manifested are stolen away. The beings of Parinirmita-Vasavartin Heaven do this for pleasure. To look at this from another perspective, your wisdom and concentration are being tested to see whether or not you can be deceived by the six desires. The meditative concentration of this heaven is also that of the Desire Realm.

Desire Realm meditative concentration is unstable. Concentration is easily lost due to scattering and agitation or sleepy grogginess, and so it is also called electro-optical concentration. You often say that this person entered samadhi, or that person entered samadhi. You are all deceiving yourselves. At best, they have merely achieved meditative concentration of the Desire Realm. Like lightning, it will be over in one instant. If you can maintain a continuous state of meditative concentration, a "singular state of mind," you will have attained true meditative stability, dhyana.

If you really attain dhyana, you will have gone beyond the limits of the Desire Realm. The first dhyana is already within the Form Realm, and is a state of joy. The first dhyana is a "singular state of mind, in which leaving behind gives rise to joy". There is no need for a physical relationship between man and woman.

Starting from the physical world to the non-material world, there is no such thing as men and women. The joy there is not comparable to the sexual pleasure of men and women in the world of desire. This is a meditative state that finally has some appeal. Otherwise, sitting in the meditation hall trying your best to withstand the feeling in your legs is the "heaven of manifesting suffering!" Oh my god, gritting your teeth, that is the "heaven of teeth gnashing," the "heaven of extreme suffering," where one is swept away by suffering.

Understanding all this, let's return to our meditation practice. Why should you practice the White Skeleton Method and Anapanasati?

The White Skeleton Method, including meditation on the body's impurities, is intended to get rid you of the view of the body as self, rid you of your attachment to this body, attachment to the five desires, such as color, sound, fragrance, touch, and to many such views. These practices are all based on this body.

Anapanasati is cultivation based on observing the great element of wind. The element of wind is the fundamental basis of the eight consciousnesses (vijnana) talked about in the Mind-only School[11]. The eight consciousnesses are fundamentally

---

[11] Also known as *Vijñapti-mātra* or *Citta-mātra* in the Yogācāra philosophy.

dependent on, this life is dependent on, breath. If you don't rely on the fundamentals to solve the problems, you will not be able to attain samadhi. The emergence of the physical world is also based the wind wheel, which you can understand by studying the Surangama Sutra. As soon as thought moves, qi will follow. Following this, the four great elements all proceed forth, and all manner of feelings, thoughts, and realms result. Conversely, if your thoughts really stop and you are singularly focused, you will transform the body of the four great elements!

Practicing Anapanasati and the White Skeleton Method will first transform your four elements. Through the wind element and Qi, your earth, water, fire, and wind elements, your habit energy, and every cell and nerve can be transformed. Only when the karmic body is transformed and you surpass all of the states of the Desire Realm will you truly achieve dhyana. I am telling you this big principle simply and clearly. This is why I tell you to put effort into practicing Anapanasati, to start with the Hinayana practices.

Buddhism is a scientific system that teaches the path of cultivation, based on fundamental truths connected with life science. If you don't understand this, all Buddhist studies are done for nothing, and all meditation is for nothing. It doesn't matter if you learn Tantra or Zen or any sect, it is useless.

Hu Songnian, this time I can only answer your questions to this extent and tell you the main points. If you want to hear about things in detail, you cannot just come once a year, imploring me to talk about it immediately and then leaving after only a short time. I will describe this in four words, "truth peddling, prajna wholesale," haha...

We'll talk about the other small side issues another time. I'm very happy you are here, so I gave this talk for you. As for the next time you come to Miaogang, this will not be the case. It will be formal classes and formal practice. Whether with the old or the young, an old relationship should not be taken casually. This is how it will be in the future.

Now I want you all to discuss what you learned! You all talk, I will just listen. Don't bother me with any more questions. You always tell me to take a rest and then you talk to me. Always telling me, "Teacher take rest," which means you want me to go away. I am not going away, and I don't want you to move. What kind of courtesy is this? You have no prajna wisdom at all!